T4-AKL-719

FACULTY / STAFF NONRENEWAL AND DISMISSAL FOR CAUSE IN INSTITUTIONS OF HIGHER EDUCATION

By Joseph C. Beckham

The Higher Education Administration Series
Edited by Donald D. Gehring and D. Parker Young

COLLEGE ADMINISTRATION PUBLICATIONS, INC.

© 1986 College Administration Publications, Inc.,
All rights reserved. Published 1986
Printed in the United States of America
90 89 88 87 86   5 4 3 2 1

Library of Congress Cataloging in Publication Data
Beckham, Joseph.
    Faculty or staff dismissal for cause in institutions.

    (The higher education administration series)
    Includes bibliographical references.
        1. College teachers—Legal status, laws, etc.—United
States.   2. College teachers—Tenure—United States.
I. Title.   II. Series.
KF4240.B43   1985   344.73'078   86-18767
ISBN 0-912557-06-0   347.30478

The views expressed in this book are those of the individual
authors and are not necessarily those of College Administration
Publications, Inc.

This publication is designed to provide accurate and
authoritative information in regard to the subject matter
covered. It is sold with the understanding that the publisher is
not engaged in rendering legal, accounting or other professional
service. If legal advice or other expert assistance is required, the
services of a competent professional person should be sought.

*—from a Declaration of Principles jointly adopted by a committee of the
American Bar Association and a committee of publishers.*

Table of Contents

Foreword

In today's litigious society, no decisions made by higher education administrators are more fraught with the potential for law suits than those decisions concerning non-renewal and dismissal for cause. The individual administrator is not shielded from being personally liable when an employee's rights have been violated by the administrator. Therefore, it is absolutely imperative that educators know the legal parameters within which they may make decisions and take actions relative to dismissal and non-retention for cause.

This monograph presents a succinct overview of the legal parameters regarding non-retention and dismissal for cause. Although Dr. Beckham has had extensive experience as an attorney and a higher education administrator, he has written the monograph in everyday language for the lay reader. The information presents a very concise review of the most up-to-date case law on the subject.

This monograph will be of value to all educators who in anyway whatsoever are involved in decisions and actions regarding non-renewal and dismissal for cause. It will also be of value to college and university faculty who need accurate and up-to-date information regarding the scope of their employment. Finally, this monograph has been prepared with the purpose of increasing knowledge and decreasing litigation.

DDG
DPY
Series Editors
September, 1986

About the Author

JOSEPH C. BECKHAM is an attorney and member of the faculty of Florida State University's College of Education. A graduate of Florida's Holland Law Center, he has served for over twelve years as a consultant and legal counselor on matters of law and education to school districts, institutions of higher education, state departments of education, and various national organizations. Prior to completion of the Ph.D. in educational administration, he was counsel to Connecticut Lieutenant Governor Peter Cashman, state director of a comprehensive educational program for Connecticut juvenile offenders and a member of two legislative task forces which drafted legislation reorganizing programs serving the educational needs of Connecticut young people.

Formerly a graduate faculty member and policy consultant with the University of Pennsylvania's Higher Education Finance Research Institute, Dr. Beckham is now an associate professor of educational leadership at Florida State University and law editor of the *Journal of Education Finance.* His legal research studies have been published in law reviews and numerous professional education journals including the *Journal of Education Finance* and the *Journal of Law and Education.* Dr. Beckham is an editor of *The Schools and the Courts.* He annually reviews appellate decisions involving public schools for the *Yearbook of School Law* and Educational Research Services series on *School Officials and the Courts.* His recent publications include an edited book entitled *Legal Issues in Public School Employment* (Bloomington, Indiana: Phi Delta Kappa Foundation, 1983) and a monograph, *Legal Aspects of Teacher Evaluation,* published by the National Organization on Legal Problems of Education.

Among his professional associations, Dr. Beckham holds membership in the American and Florida Bar Associations and the National

Association of College and University Attorneys. He has served as a member of the Board of Directors of the National Organization on Legal Problems of Education and was selected by Phi Delta Kappa as one of the nation's Outstanding Young Education Leaders in celebration of that professional education association's seventy-fifth anniversary.

Chapter I

Introduction

Employees of a higher education institution are subject to dismissal for cause, but legal and institutional standards for determining "cause" are varied. Incompetence,[1] neglect of duty,[2] insubordination,[3] immorality or unethical conduct,[4] have been the most prevalent bases for such dismissals, yet these terms are ambiguous and subject to conflicting interpretation in particular circumstances.

A definition of "adequate" cause will often depend on the policy and practices of a particular institution. Formulating definitions will require a balance between institutional mission and professional "best practice" as articulated by institutional faculty and staff. General agreement may be difficult to obtain, but a standard that provides a basis for fair proceedings and permits adequate documentation is crucial to the employment decision-making process.

Courts are not arbiters of standards for professional practice in higher education, but judicial opinion can contribute to an understanding of what constitutes legally sound, fair, and reasonable policy in cases involving dismissal or retention of faculty and staff. The analysis of court cases which follows is designed to inform the employment practice of institutions of higher education, not as an unerring guide, but as a compendium of instances in which institutional procedures and practices were scrutinized and a legal standard of varying generalizability was adopted.

JUDICIAL REVIEW

Judicial opinion emphasizes that termination for cause involves determination of professional competency that is "peculiarly within

---

[1]Chung v. Park, 514 F. 2d 382 (3rd Cir. 1975).
[2]Shaw v. Board of Trustees of Frederick Community College, 549 F. 2d 929 (4th Cir. 1976).
[3]State ex rel. Richardson v. Board of Regents, 269 P. 2d 265 (Nev. 1954).
[4]Koch v. Board of Trustees of Univ. of Illinois, 187 N.E. 2d 340 (Ill. App. 1963), *cert. denied*, 375 U.S. 989 (1964).

1

the discretion of a college administrator."[5] As such, these decisions are subject to judicial review on relatively narrow grounds, limited by the judiciary's awareness that intrusion into the realm of academic decision-making is beyond the expertise of judges.[6] The wisdom of an institution's employment decision is less susceptible to challenge because of this judicial deference to academic decision-makers, however, the fairness of that decision, particularly the assessment of procedural safeguards and the requirement of substantial evidence to support adequate cause for an adverse employment decision is within the province of the courts.[7]

Substantive grounds for adequate cause dismissal have been subject to judicial review in a large number of cases. These adverse employment decisions often involve important contractual and constitutional principles, influencing institutional policies and practices at both private and public colleges and universities.[8] Cases of specified cause for dismissal are typically complex, fact-intensive, and emotionally charged. Adequate procedural standards for effecting dismissal and appropriate standards for defining and determining "cause" are critical issues.

Judicial scrutiny of substantive grounds for good cause dismissal will be predicated upon a review of the contract of employment as influenced by institutional policies and traditional practices. In public institutions, judicial review may also extend to state statutes, administrative regulations, or constitutional provisions which define employment standards or evaluation criteria. Under federal anti-discrimination statutes, public and private institutions' employment policies or practices may be subject to judicial assessment of discriminatory intent or impact.

THE EMPLOYMENT RELATIONSHIP

The employment rights of college and university faculty are determined from the principles of contract law applicable to all employment relationships. Since the contract of employment will vary on an institution to institution basis, courts must deal with challenges to a termination decision on a case by case basis. In some instances a court will be confined to the material representations in the individual contract, in other instances, a collectively negotiated agreement may

---

[5]Chung v. Park, 514 F. 2d 382, 387 (3rd Cir. 1975).
[6]See Ferguson v. Thomas, 430 F. 2d 852 (5th Cir. 1970).
[7]See Poterma v. Ping, 462 F. Supp. 328 (S.D. Ohio 1978) (impartial hearing is required in faculty termination) and Bignal v. North Idaho College, 538 F. 2d 243 (9th Cir. 1976) (termination must be supported by rational basis and made in good faith).
[8]A comprehensive review of the interaction between legal accountability and academic policy or prerogative is offered in Olswang and Lee, *Faculty Freedoms and Institutional Accountability: Interactions and Conflicts* (1984).

be the basis for contract interpretation. Particularly where ambiguities in the contract appear, a court may review various policy documents; such as faculty handbooks, memoranda of agreement, oral promises, or institutional practices, in order to interpret the nature of the employment relationship. In some instances, policy or practice external to the institution may be cited by a court as creating an academic standard applicable to the contract of employment, as when courts rely on professional standards advanced by organizations such as the American Association of University Professors (AAUP).[9]

Public institutions must provide contractual agreements that correspond to provisions of state statute law and regulation. In many instances, these statutes will delineate the length of an employment contract and define tenured status at the public institution. Faculty at public institutions also enjoy constitutional guarantees under the Fourteenth Amendment and the Bill of Rights which further constrain public employers. The Fourteenth Amendment prohibits states from depriving individuals of privileges and immunities secured by the United States Constitution and laws and requires due process of law where a denial of liberty or property is implicated. As public institutions are state agencies for purposes of the Fourteenth Amendment, any denial of employment rights guaranteed by a contractual obligation would constitute a denial of property rights that would compel due process. Alternately, if a public institution's employment decision was so stigmatizing as to foreclose other employment opportunities, a liberty interest would be implicated that would compel due process.

In the context of private higher education, verbal assurances or promises, traditional institutional practice or custom, and written personnel policies may serve as the basis for concluding that the employing institution has created a contractual obligation that extends beyond the contract of employment. When a university faculty member with six years of service under a series of term contracts was notified of nonrenewal, he sued, alleging that the university had breached a contractual obligation to provide tenure review in his sixth year of employment. The federal court agreed with the employee's theory that institutional practice, policy statements, and oral representations of supervisory employees could create an enforceable contract, but concluded that the facts did not support the claim that the institution had breached a contractual obligation to provide a tenure review.[10]

Careful review of published institutional policies in order to modify or eliminate written policy statements that afford an aggrieved em-

---

[9]*See* McKee, "Tenure by Default: the Non-Formal Acquisition of Academic Tenure," 7 *J. of C. and Univ. L.* 31-56 (1980).
[10]Marwil v. Baker, 499 *F. Supp.* 560 (E.D. Mich. 1980).

ployee a basis for asserting additional employment rights is an important element in avoiding contractual claims.[11] Typically, employment contracts incorporate by reference the institution's personnel policies. The express wording of such an incorporation may vary, but usually includes phrases such as "This contract is subject to rules, regulations and policies adopted for governance of the institution." In one instance a word processing manager successfully sued an Illinois community college district for wrongful discharge after establishing that the college's adverse employment decision violated provisions of the institution's "Administrative and Non-teaching Professional Personnel Manual," a document presumed to be incorporated in the employee's contract of employment.[12]

Institutions can mitigate an employment claim based upon the oral representations of supervisory agents by adopting and disseminating written policies which limit the institutional representatives who are authorized to give oral assurance of continuing employment. In a representative case, *Beckwith* v. *Rhode Island School of Design*,[13] a faculty member asserted reliance on his department head's statement that the faculty member would be granted a three-year contract following an initial probationary year of service. Rejecting the faculty member's claim, the court affirmed a motion to dismiss on the ground that the department head possessed no actual or apparent authority to bind the institution, nor had the institution acted to ratify the oral promise.[14]

TENURE STATUS

Tenured status, whether expressed or implied in an institution's contract of employment or specified under state laws applicable to public institutions, conveys a property right to continued employment which may be altered only for cause. Tenure is a protection against arbitrary dismissal which requires an institution to justify "adequate" cause for the adverse employment decision. While tenure is considered an entitlement that protects the faculty member's right to academic freedom, the procedural protections associated with this contractual mechanism would not prohibit dismissal for cause or termination for noncausal reasons such as financial exigency, program discontinuance or mandatory retirement.[15]

---

[11]*See* Mawdsley and Permuth, "Faculty Dismissal: Comparison of Public and Private Higher Education," *School Law Update* 138-160 (Jones and Semler, eds., 1985).

[12]Piper v. Board of Trustees, 426 *N.E.* 2d 262 (Ill. App. 1979). *But see* Sargent v. Illinois Institute of Technology, 397 *N.E.* 2d 443 (Ill. App. 1979).

[13] 404 *A.* 2d 480 (R.I. 1979).

[14]*Id.*

[15]*See* Olswang, "Planning the Unthinkable: Issues in Institutional Reorganization and Faculty Reductions," 9 *J. of C. and Univ. L.* 431-449 (1983).

Tenure may be conceptualized as a property interest in continued employment formally conveyed to the employee by the institution as a guarantee that the employee will not be dismissed absent a showing of adequate cause. Tenure provides an assurance that, following a specified period of probationary service, the employee's continued employment or academic freedom will not be jeopardized without fundamental due process protection. Van Alstyne expresses the concept of tenure as "a favorable judgment establishing a rebuttable presumption of the individual's professional excellence . . . (W)hen it can be shown that the individual possessing tenure has nonetheless fallen short or has otherwise misconducted himself as determined according to full academic due process, the presumption is lost and the individual is subject to dismissal."[16]

The United States Supreme Court has recognized that tenure or continuing contract status creates a protected property right worthy of due process protection in public institutions of higher education. In *Perry* v. *Sindermann*,[17] the Court ruled that a community college faculty member who held his position for four years under the institution's de facto tenure policy could establish a legitimate claim of entitlement that would require due process prior to termination. The professor's reliance upon statements in the institution's faculty handbook and oral promises of supervisory administrators created his entitlement to tenure. Once recognized, such an entitlement would assure a faculty member the right to notice and a hearing at which the institution could be compelled to justify dismissal on the basis of adequate cause.

TERM CONTRACT

A requirement of adequate cause would also apply to term contracts of provisional faculty or staff if the institution sought to dismiss the employee prior to the effective date of contract termination. A public employee dismissed during the term of a contract and in breach of its provisions has a legitimate claim of entitlement and a property interest in continued employment worthy of due process protection.[18] If an institution simply elects not to renew an employment contract, proper notice of contract expiration would leave the employee with no basis for asserting a legitimate expectancy of continued employment under the contract. Under these circumstances, the decision not to renew the contract would not require an institution to establish adequate cause for its employment decision.[19]

---

[16]Van Alstyne, "Tenure: A Summary, Explanation and 'Defense,'" in *ASHE Reader on Faculty and Faculty Issues in Colleges and Universities* 146-150, 147 (Finkelstein, ed., 1985).
[17]408 *U.S.* 593 (1972).
[18]Vanelli v. Reynolds School Dist., 667 *F.* 2d 773 (9th Cir. 1982).
[19]Board of Regents v. Roth, 408 *U.S.* 564 (1972).

Compliance with contractual terms and applicable state laws in any decision not to renew a provisional employee would eliminate the necessity for a showing of adequate cause for non-renewal. Courts have adopted the view that, absent a showing of discriminatory animus or an intent to deprive the employee of protected constitutional rights, an institution may refuse to renew a contract of employment without risk of judicial intervention.[20] In *Perry* the Court cautioned that if the employee had no contractual or other claim to job tenure, his claim would be defeated.[21] Absent a public employer's action to terminate based upon a desire to penalize the employee's exercise of constitutional rights or invidiously discriminate, the non-tenured employee could not compel due process on expiration of the employment agreement.

AT-WILL STATUS

An employee who is hired for an indefinite term is generally regarded as being "terminable at will" without any requirement that the institution establish adequate cause or give any reason for its decision.[22] Typically faculty at institutions of higher education enjoy some protection in their employment as faculty members, either by virtue of tenured status or through term contract guarantees. "At-will" status more often applies to staff members whose contracts do not specify a requirement of "cause" for dismissal and who are given no definite period of guaranteed employment.

Discharge of an "at-will" employee need not be accompanied by a finding of cause for dismissal. At-will employees have no property interest in continued employment beyond the terms of their contract and can be terminated upon reasonable notice. However, the at-will employee terminated in retaliation for the exercise of a constitutional right or for an impermissible reason (e.g., race discrimination) may assert a claim of wrongful discharge as a bar to termination.[23] For example, a nurse anesthetist at a university hospital won damages for wrongful discharge when it was determined she was terminated because she refused to give false testimony in a medical malpractice suit against her employer.[24]

ACADEMIC FREEDOM

A traditional faculty right protected through the tenure mechanism is the prerogative of academic freedom. In 1940, the AAUP pro-

---

[20]*See* Hetrick v. Martin, 480 *F.* 2d 705 (6th Cir. 1973) (use of subjective evaluation in recommendation not to renew) and Stebbins v. Weaver, 537 *F.* 2d 939 (7th Cir. 1976) (no evidence of discriminatory animus in decision not to renew employee).

[21]408 *U.S.* at 602 n. 7.

[22]*See* Hustoles, "Faculty and Staff Dismissals: Developing Contract and Tort Theories," 10 *J. of C. and Univ. L.* 479-494 (1983).

[23]Rossi v. Pennsylvania State Univ., 489 *A.* 2d 828 (Pa. Sup. 1985).

[24]Sides v. Duke Hospital, 328 *So.* 2d 818 (N.C. App. 1985).

mulgated its "Statement of Principles on Academic Freedom and Tenure" which states in part:

(a) The teacher is entitled to full freedom in research and in the publication of the results, subject to the adequate performance of his other academic duties; but research for pecuniary return should be based upon an understanding with the authorities of the institution.

(b) The teacher is entitled to freedom in the classroom in discussing his subject, but he should be careful not to introduce into his teaching controversial matter which has no relation to his subject. Limitations of academic freedom because of religious or other aims of the institution should be clearly stated in writing at the time of the appointment.

(c) The college or university teacher is a citizen, a member of a learned profession, and an officer of an educational institution. When he speaks or writes as a citizen, he should be free from institutional censorship or discipline, but his special position in the community imposes special obligations. As a man of learning and an educational officer, he should remember that the public may judge his profession and his institution by his utterances. Hence he should at all times be accurate, should exercise appropriate restraint, should show respect for the opinions of others, and should make every effort to indicate that he is not an institutional spokesman.[25]

In *Sweezey* v. *New Hampshire*,[26] the United States Supreme Court emphasized a university professor's right to academic freedom in overturning a contempt order directed at a tenured professor who refused to answer a legislative investigation committee's questions concerning his political activities, opinions and beliefs. Chief Justice Warren's opinion on behalf of the Court's majority included the following observation.

The essentiality of freedom in the community of American universities is almost self-evident. No one should underestimate the vital role in a democracy that is played by those who guide and train our youth. To impose any strait jacket upon the intellectual leaders in our colleges and universities would imperil the future of our Nation. No field of education is so thoroughly comprehended by man that new discoveries cannot yet be made. Particularly is that true in the social sciences, where few, if any, principles are accepted as absolutes. Scholarship cannot flourish in an atmosphere of suspicion and distrust. Teachers and students must always remain free to inquire, to study and to evaluate, to gain new maturity and understanding; otherwise our civilization will stagnate and die.[27]

While courts have recognized academic freedom as a protection against arbitrary dismissal based upon a faculty member's expression

---

[25]As quoted in *Academic Freedom and Tenure* 33-36, 35 (Joughlin, ed., 1969).
[26]354 *U.S.* 234 (1957).
[27]*Id.* at 250 (emphasis added).

7

or inquiry, academic freedom would not appear to protect a faculty member's failure to follow institutional rules or directives or an employee's exercise of free speech which was a material interference or substantial disruption in the institution's operation.[28] In one case, a faculty member refused to disclose information related to his vote as a committee member considering promotion of a female associate professor, claiming an academic freedom privilege against court ordered disclosure of the information in a case in which the associate professor alleged sex discrimination. The Fifth Circuit Court of Appeals rejected the academic freedom evidentiary defense and upheld a contempt order of the lower federal court taking the view that academic freedom did not extend to the confidentiality of such communications.[29]

PUBLIC / PRIVATE DISTINCTIONS

The law distinguishes between public and private institutions for purposes of regulation and enforcement of state and federal statutory and constitutional standards. Public institutions are subject to the constraints of the United States Constitution, particularly the provisions of the First and Fourteenth Amendments, while private institutions are not so constrained. The Constitution, as a limitation on the powers of state and federal authorities, is applicable to institutions which are public in the sense that they are subsidized and governed by the state, or otherwise engaged in state action through the acts or representations of their agents and employees. Private institutions may be subject to federal and state regulation in specific circumstances, but are not prohibited from restricting freedoms such as free speech, association, equal protection or due process. While an ostensibly private institution may be held to be engaged in state action for purposes of liability for the denial of constitutional rights, it is generally the case that private institutions are not subject to these federal constitutional constraints.[30]

Private institutions may be subject to a range of federal and state statutory and administrative regulations depending on their participation in federal and state subsidy programs. For example, institutions receiving federal financial assistance may be required to comply with regulations related to federal antidiscrimination statutes. In addition, a wide range of common law standards, slowly emerging in the area of employment rights, may ultimately compel private institutions to adopt employment policies and practices that harmonize with public institutions governed by constitutional mandates.[31]

[28]Jawa v. Fayetteville State University, 426 *F. Supp.* 218 (E.D. N.C. 1976).
[29]In re Dinnan, 661 *F.* 2d 426 (5th Cir. 1981), cert. denied, 457 *U.S.* 1106 (1982).
[30]See Thigpen, "The Application of Fourteenth Amendment Norms to Private Colleges and Universities," 11 *J. of L. and Educ.* 171 (1982).
[31]See Histoles, "Faculty and Staff Dismissals: Developing Contract and Tort Theories," 10 *J. of C. and Univ. L.* 479-494 (1983-84).

OVERBREADTH OR VAGUENESS

In the development and implementation of adequate cause standards for public institutions of higher education, definitions of what constitutes "adequate cause" should be elaborated with sufficient particularity to enable reasonable persons to agree on commonly held notions of proscribed conduct within the profession. As one authority has noted, these definitions "should be sufficiently clear to guide the decision-makers who will apply them and to forewarn the faculty members who will be subject to them."[32] It is equally important that the adequate cause standards relate to professional fitness, as institutions may be required to bear the burden of persuading judges that a faculty or staff member's conduct has a detrimental effect on institutional efficiency.

A faculty and staff handbook or other provision citing an adequate cause standard for dismissal may be regarded as void if it fails to clarify the meaning which is to be attached to the applicable standard of adequate cause.[33] Under standards advocated by the AAUP, "adequate cause" for dismissal must be related to a faculty member's fitness "in his professional capacity as a teacher or researcher."[34] Further, the AAUP suggests that adequate cause be restricted to "demonstrated incompetence or dishonesty in teaching or research, substantial and manifest neglect of duty, or personal conduct which substantially impairs the individual's fulfillment of his institutional responsibilities.[35] While a faculty and staff handbook might recognize dismissal for "adequate cause" a challenge that the provision was overbroad and thus violated First Amendment free speech and association or was so vague as to violate due process under the Fourteenth Amendment might be sustained if institutional officials failed to elaborate the bases for adequate cause as it related to professional fitness.[36]

In *Keyishian* v. *Board of Regents*,[37] the United States Supreme Court considered a challenge by faculty dismissed for refusing to sign a certificate stating they were not and had never been Communists. The certificates were incorporated as a condition of employment in a recently merged state university. In concluding that the dismissals violated First Amendment rights to freedom of association, the Court

---

[32] Kaplan, *The Law of Higher Education* 166-67 (2nd ed. 1985).

[33] *See* Tuma v. Board of Nursing, 593 P. 2d 711 (Idaho 1979) (suspension for "unprofessional conduct" invalid) and Davis v. Williams, 598 F. 2d 916 (5th Cir. 1979) (regulation prohibiting "conduct prejudicial to good order" invalid).

[34] Recommended Institutional Regulations on Academic Freedom and Tenure, 62 *AAUP Bulletin* 184 (1976).

[35] *Id.*

[36] *But See* Garrett v. Matthews, 625 F. 2d 658 (5th Cir. 1980). A tenured professor's claim that the standard of "adequate cause" was unconstitutionally vague was dismissed by the federal court of appeals.

[37] 385 *U.S.* 589 (1967).

found the certificate requirement overbroad. Since membership alone would not be enough to establish an intent to further unlawful aims, the Court held the exclusion from employment was impermissible.[38] Further, the uncertainty about what is proscribed by the law would stifle dialogue and, in reference to the linkage between academic freedom and First Amendment rights, "cast a pall of orthodoxy over the classroom . . ."[39]

In *Adamian* v. *Jacobsen*,[40] a professor challenged the university code provision requiring faculty "to exercise appropriate restraint [and] show respect for the opinions of others." On review of a decision to dismiss the employee for his alleged role in leading a disruptive demonstration on the campus, a federal appeals court remanded the case for a determination of how the university interpreted and applied the code provisions. In the appellate court's view, only a narrow interpretation and application of the code provision would avoid a holding that the code was void as overbroad. In essence, the federal appeals court insisted the lower court assess whether the code as interpreted and applied was sufficiently specific to preclude dismissal for an unpopular yet constitutionally protected exercise of free speech.

On remand, a federal district court upheld the dismissal because the university governing board had interpreted the university code provision in a manner consistent with that given the provision by the AAUP. In affirming that holding, the Ninth Circuit found no violation of free speech and association under the First Amendment.[41] The AAUP interpretation asserted that the provision was not directed at the substance of a teacher's remarks and could only be invoked when the remarks raised grave doubts concerning a teacher's fitness for his position. The appeals court concluded the AAUP had so narrowed the language of the section that any substantive overbreadth had been eliminated. Since the regents in interpreting this same section agreed with the AAUP construction, the section was not unconstitutionally overbroad. The appellate court agreed with the trial court's findings and conclusions that the professor's activities were beyond the mere advocacy of ideas and counseled a course of action, which interfered with the regular operation of the school, outside the protection of the First Amendment.[42]

Public institutions have successfully overcome a vagueness challenge to "adequate cause" standards by adopting the AAUP "Statement on Professional Ethics" and incorporating the statement in the

---

[38]*Id.* at 601.
[39]*Id.* 603.
[40]523 *F.* 2d 929 (9th Cir. 1975).
[41]Adamian v. Lombardi, 608 *F.* 2d 1224 (9th Cir. 1979).
[42]*Id.*

10

Faculty Handbook. In one case, a faculty member, alleged to have made sexual advances toward male students, was dismissed under an ethics provision which prohibited exploitation of students and required professors to respect students and adhere to a proper role as a counselor. In rejecting the professor's claim that the dismissal violated due process because the provision was unconstitutionally vague, a federal appeals court determined that an institution need not specify every type of impermissible conduct as long as interpretation of what is unacceptable conduct is consistent with reasonable professional standards and capable of being understood by the faculty member.[43]

SUMMARY

Defining standards of adequate cause to which faculty and staff may be held accountable is the prerogative of an institution of higher education. The institution may provide for dismissal on the basis of affirmative misconduct and on the basis that the employee has failed to meet a specified norm of productivity or performance. However, ambiguity in the standards for adequate cause, as those standards are applied in specific cases, may compel judicial intervention to insure fundamental fairness, reasonableness and procedural compliance with the terms and conditions of the employment contract.

Despite judicial deference to administrative decision-making in cases of dismissal for cause, an adverse employment decision may compel judicial scrutiny where valued property rights, such as tenure, or faculty prerogatives, such as academic freedom, are at issue. In this context, public institutions are particularly vulnerable to suit because these institutions are constrained by federal constitutional law. However, even the ostensibly private college or university may be liable for a denial of constitutional rights if it can be established that the institution is engaged in state action. Both public and private institutions are governed by state and federal regulatory standards that apply to the employment relationship, and it is argued that the traditional distinctions between the legal responsibilities of these institutions have blurred.

The development and implementation of adequate cause standards is critical to both public and private institutions. Private institutions are legally vulnerable when ambiguities or misstatements in the contract of employment can be utilized by an aggrieved employee. Public institutions may be accused of invoking standards which are void due to First Amendment "over-breadth" or Fourteenth Amendment "vagueness" challenges.

---

[43]Korf v. Ball State Univ., 726 F. 2d 1222 (7th Cir. 1984). *See* Arnett v. Kennedy, 416 U.S. 134 (1974) in which the United States Supreme Court sustained a provision authorizing dismissal of a federal employee for "such cause as will promote the efficiency of the service" at 158.

Judicial opinion in cases involving adverse employment decisions can be surveyed for the purpose of extrapolating legal principles applicable to college and university administration. While these opinions do not offer a concise guide to best professional practice, the case law does offer illustrative examples that can inform employment decision-making involving faculty and staff. In the analysis that follows, case law provides the primary basis for generalizations about the legal aspects of employee dismissal and retention in colleges and universities.

Chapter II

Adequate Cause for Dismissal

Tenure or term contract provisions typically specify or incorporate by reference a number of grounds for termination. When an employment contract is involved, as in the case of tenured faculty or a staff member dismissed prior to the end of the contract term, these grounds constitute a basis for establishing the employee's breach of the contractual obligation. If the institution can present evidence to support adequate or good cause for dismissal, then the institution may alter the employment contract by dismissal of the employee, reprimand, suspension, or other adverse employment decision.

Among the substantive grounds most often mentioned as constituting adequate cause are "incompetency," "neglect of duty," "insubordination," "immorality," or "unethical conduct."[1] Institutional regulations should make explicit the procedures necessary for dismissal and list standards or criteria upon which the action can be based,[2] but the nature and specificity of these provisions will vary from institution to institution.

Absence of a specific definition of adequate cause or lack of evidence to support adequate cause has led courts to consider challenges to adverse employment decisions on a case-by-case basis. Imprecise definitions compel courts to make determinations based on elusive standards. As a consequence, notions of what constitutes adequate cause are governed largely by a piecemeal examination of case law extrapolating evidentiary standards and operational definitions on a case-by-case, state-by-state, institution-by-institution basis.

In assessing substantive grounds for dismissal and determining whether the institution has established adequate cause, courts are prin-

---

[1]See Lovain, "Grounds for Dismissing Tenured Postsecondary Faculty for Cause, 10 J. of C. and Univ. L. 419-433 (1983).

[2]See Bickel, "Termination of Faculty," 11 NOLPE School L. J. 30 (1983). The author discusses faculty termination in the context of program discontinuance and financial exigency.

cipally concerned with the effect on the employee's ability to perform duties and the institution's capacity to provide educational services. In many instances the court will consider whether the employee's conduct has a cognizable detrimental effect on the performance of assigned duties. Whether the basis for dismissal focuses on some affirmative action by the employee or on the employee's failure to meet a requisite standard of professional fitness, dismissal is proper when the conduct makes the employee less effective in his or her job than is necessary for the institution to maintain its educational standards or operate efficiently and effectively.

The detrimental effect test provides a framework through which substantive grounds for dismissal of faculty and staff can be understood and applied. In assessing adequate cause for dismissal, the test focuses on the consequence of employee conduct as that conduct influences the institution's overall ability to realize its educational mission. In the case analyses that follow, the utility of the detrimental effect test will be illustrated in its application to faculty or staff dismissal for cause at colleges and universities. In some instances, analogous cases from public school settings will be utilized to augment and elaborate the applicable legal standards.

INCOMPETENCY

The detrimental effect test would require dismissal of a faculty or staff member for incompetence if a substantial and specific lack of ability renders the employee unable to effectively perform the teaching or other duties imposed by the employing institution. The employee's incompetency must be so acute that remediation is impossible within a reasonable period of time or the employee's attitude so recalcitrant as to indicate unwillingness to make necessary changes. The institution should establish the specific knowledge or skill found lacking and the standards and procedures used to identify the alleged incompetence so that the employee is adequately informed of the deficiency.

A functional standard for employee dismissal in incompetency cases, one which will withstand judicial scrutiny under a detrimental effect test, requires two steps. First, the institution must identify in advance the knowledge, skills, or competencies it requires. Second, the institution must develop evaluative mechanisms for identifying incompetence through documentation of deficiencies. Faculty and staff must be adequately informed of the standards they must meet and provided with a reasonable opportunity to correct deficiencies once identified. This two-step process will ensure compliance with the standard most frequently expressed in the case law—that the conduct that

14

occasioned the dismissal evince an inability to perform the duties assigned and an incapability to function effectively in the role prescribed by the institution. The governing board need not continue an employee whose methods are ineffective or whose attitude is improper if his or her retention will directly harm students or otherwise impair the institution's pursuit of its educational mission.

Incompetency dismissals are subject to heightened judicial scrutiny largely because institutions frequently lack defensible data on which to base evaluations of performance. Employees typically challenge these dismissals, asserting insufficient evidence for the adverse employment decision. Judicial use of the detrimental effect test in incompetency cases has emphasized the appraisal of employee performance which can be said to have a bearing on the student's opportunity to learn or the employee's ability to perform institutional responsibilities. While a faculty member's performance may relate to matters other than teaching, reasons successfully put forth in court reviewed determinations of teacher incompetency include lack of knowledge of subject matter,[4] lack of proper organization of classroom time,[5] and inadequate development of lesson plans.[6] In addition, a teacher's failure to adapt instructional procedures[7] or coordinate teaching with that of colleagues[8] have been accepted as reasons for dismissal based on incompetence.

Chung v. *Park*[9] is an often cited legal precedent which emphasizes the discretion of college authorities in making termination decisions and elaborates the importance of balancing institutional versus individual employee interests in the case of termination. Professor Chung was notified he would not be renewed while in his fifth year of teaching at Mansfield State College. The college administration advised Chung that his intransigence in dealing with superiors and unfavorable evaluations by students and faculty had led to the decision not to renew. Chung had been given previous notice of specific deficiencies, but there was no evidence he had attempted to improve his performance.

---

[3]*See* Olswang and Fantel, "Tenure and Periodic Performance Review: Compatible Legal and Administrative Principles," 7 *J. of C. and Univ. L.* 1 (1981) and Stroup, "Faculty Evaluation," in *Issues in Faculty Personnel Policies* (Fuller, ed., 1983).
[4]*See* United States v. South Carolina, 445 *F. Supp.* 1094 (D.S.C. 1977), *aff'd* 434 *U.S.* 1026 (1978).
[5]Community Unit School Dist. v. Maclin, 435 *N.E.* 2d 845 (Ill. App. 1982).
[6]Carson City School Dist. v. Bernsen, 608 *P.* 2d 507 (Nev. 1980).
[7]Rosso v. Board of School Dirs., 380 *A.* 2d 1328 (Pa. Commw. 1977).
[8]LaBorde v. Regents, Univ. of California, 495 *F. Supp.* 1067 (C.D. Cal. 1980) and Jawa v. Fayetteville State Univ., 426 *F. Supp.* 218 (E.D. N.C. 1976). Difficulty in working with co-workers is often presumed by courts to implicate ineffective performance in the classroom. *See* Grant v. Board of Educ. of School Dirs., 417 *A.* 2d 1292 (Pa. Commw. 1984) and Yielding v. Crockett Independent School Dist., 707 *F.* 2d 196 (5th Cir. 1983).
[9]514 *F.* 2d 382 (3rd Cir. 1975), *cert. denied*, 423 *U.S.* 948 (1975).

Following the termination notice, Chung sought and received a termination hearing at which a local attorney and two professors teaching at other colleges heard his claim that his termination was unreasonable, arbitrary and capricious. The hearing panel permitted Chung to be represented by counsel, to cross-examine adverse witnesses, present evidence, and obtain a transcript of the proceedings. Chung argued that he was denied procedural due process when he was given notice of termination without being afforded a hearing before the decision to terminate.

In concluding that the determination of professional competency is a matter within the discretion of a college administration, the Third Circuit Court of Appeals reviewed Chung's claim and found for the college.[10] The hearing Chung received was provided after the decision to terminate, but it was still a pretermination hearing since Chung continued to receive job benefits as a faculty member. The court balanced the professor's interest in avoiding an unreasonable termination against the college's interest in insuring an efficient process for terminating incompetent faculty and ruled in favor of the institution, noting, in particular, that the record of Chung's unsatisfactory job performance supported the decision to terminate.[11]

A faculty member's effect on students is an important index in assessing detrimental effect. Dismissals have been upheld for unreasonably harsh or arbitrary treatment of students,[12] including the use of unprovoked, unwarranted and highly improper forms of punishment or implementation of a philosophy of grading inconsistent with stated guidelines for evaluating and grading student progress.[13] In *Jawa v. Fayetteville State University*,[14] a tenured professor was dismissed on charges of lack of class preparation, poor teaching, and poor relations with students. In response to a challenge to dismissal brought on civil rights grounds, a federal district court concluded the university had established sufficient evidence of incompetence to justify dismissal.[15]

Similarly, a staff or faculty member's interactions with co-workers can be evaluated in assessing detrimental effect. A Pennsylvania school psychologist, with duties that included diagnostic evaluation of special education students for purposes of placement and consultation with parents and school personnel on recommendations for placement, was properly dismissed for incompetence after notice and a hearing.

---

[10]*Id.*

[11]*Id.* at 385.

[12]*See* Donnes v. State, 672 *P.* 2d 617 (Mont. 1983) (abusive and arbitrary treatment of students) and Fay v. Board of Dirs. of North-Linn, 298 *N.W.* 2d 345 (Iowa App. 1980) (harassment and lack of rapport).

[13]*See* Whaley v. Anoka-Hennepin Independent School Dist., 325 *N.W.* 2d 128 (Minn. 1982).

[14]426 *F. Supp.* 218 (E.D. N.C. 1976).

[15]*Id.* at 229.

Although periodic evaluations had not been undertaken, the record disclosed that during the last year of her employment the psychologist was unable to induce any of her co-workers to co-sign her reports because they lacked meaningful content and quality. The psychologist, in testing for special education placement, failed to make appropriate placement decisions. Testimony by peers and the supervisor provided details of instances in which it become apparent the psychologist was indifferent to these problems when they were brought to her attention. The supervisor's testimony elaborated unrebutted instances of inadequate reports, improper testing procedures, ill-considered placement recommendations, and noncontribution in conference.[16]

Incompetency may extend to issues of mental and emotional fitness. A tenured public school teacher with an entitlement to due process under Illinois law was found not to meet the medical standard for teaching following a psychiatric evaluation. The evaluation was compelled by the school superintendent after an investigation by the teacher's school principal led the principal to request the health examination. The teacher had complained that a student in his class sought to disrupt the class and turn other students against him. The principal requested that the teacher put his observations in a written memorandum and then used the memorandum as the basis for requesting the evaluation.

As a result of the evaluation, the teacher was told that dismissal would be recommended if he failed to request a leave of absence. The teacher chose the leave, but later contended that he had been compelled to leave his position and denied due process. The court held that no due process denial occurred when the teacher exercised the option of a leave rather than defend himself in a proper dismissal hearing.[17]

Incompetency as a basis for dismissal must incorporate charges and an evidentiary record which documents and validates the charges. A tenured faculty member had urged his students not to take northern Wisconsin teaching jobs and opposed a graduate program where graduate students were permitted to take courses offered as a part of a bachelor's degree program. Dismissal was overturned as the allegations did not support incompetency as the stated grounds for dismissal and would more appropriately be related to insubordinate conduct.[18]

NEGLECT OF DUTY

Faculty and staff are charged with express and implied obligations under the contract of employment. The faculty member's duties

---

[16]Grant v. Board of Education of Centennial, 417 A. 2d 1292 (Pa. Commw. 1984).
[17]Dusanek v. Hannon, 677 F. 2d 538 (7th Cir. 1982).
[18]State v. McPhee, 94 N.W. 2d 711 (Wis. 1959).

may extend beyond teaching to requirements related to service and research. Institutional requirements for reporting, committee work, maintenance of office hours and other obligations of the employment relationship are enforceable elements of performance. When these duties are shown to be job-related, failure to meet a specific duty can serve as a basis for dismissal, provided that the detrimental effect of a failure to perform can be documented or persuasively argued by the institution.

Dismissal for neglect of duty has been justified in instances of excessive absence or tardiness,[19] failure to meet professional growth requirements essential for continued employment[20] and failure to maintain office hours.[21] Tenured faculty have lost their jobs after failing to appear for work at the appointed time, leading reviewing courts to conclude faculty members had voluntarily abandoned their property interests in continued employment.[22]

In a case which reflects the elements of neglect of duty, a community college successfully justified nonreappointment of a mathematics department chairman on the basis that he failed to implement a required evaluation of his administrative performance. The college handbook called for comprehensive evaluation of employee performance prior to the end of each term contract and the chair's written agreement with the college specified evaluation as a basis for consideration of another contract term. An Oregon appeals court held the relevant college rule to mean that the department chairman is responsible for the designation of the person to conduct the evaluation and, by implication, is similarly responsible for the appropriate completion of the evaluation, as a condition precedent to reappointment.[23] Finding that the plaintiff had not satisfied this responsibility, the court found he was not in a position to complain of his nonreappointment.[24]

Failure to complete and submit project reports and to observe institutional rules for reporting and accounting for expenditure of funds can be considered as evidence of neglect of duty. In one instance, a tenured faculty member failed to report, consistent with university

---

[19]*See* Willis v. School Dist. of Kansas City, 606 *S.W.* 2d 189 (Mo. App. 1980) (absence to participate in illegal strike) and Board of Educ. of Tempe v. Lammle, 596 *P.* 2d 48 (Ariz. App. 1979). *See Also* Stastny v. Board of Trustees of Central Washington Univ., 647 *P.* 2d 496 (Wash. App. 1982), *cert. denied* 103 *S.Ct.* 1528 (1982) (record of previous absences supported termination for failure to attend classes after being directed to do so).
[20]Turney v. Alread Public Schools, 666 *S.W.* 2d 687 (Ark. 1984); Harrah Independent School Dist. v. Martin, 440 *U.S.* 194 (1979); and Last v. Board of Educ., 37 Ill. App. 2d 159 (1962).
[21]Jawa v. Fayetteville State Univ., 426 *F. Supp.* 218 (E.D. N.C. 1976).
[22]Kalme v. West Virginia Board of Regents, 539 *F.* 2d 1346, 1348 (4th Cir. 1976); Akyeampong v. Coppin State College, 538 *F. Supp.* 986, 990 (D. Md. 1982).
[23]Zink v. Lane Community College, 578 *P.* 2d 471 (Or. App. 1978).
[24]*Id.* at 474.

regulation, on sponsored research grants and was dismissed after an opportunity for review before a faculty grievance committee. The committee rejected the faculty member's contention that his failure to report was a protest of university accounting policy. On appeal to a federal district court, the dismissal was affirmed.[25]

Contract termination, based upon charges of violating school district rules and neglect of duty, was upheld in a case in which a public school teacher failed to report lost or damaged books in a timely fashion and destroyed final examination papers in violation of school district policy. While each instance, taken alone, might seem trivial, the Supreme court of Arkansas noted that the directives were clearly communicated and reasonable, concluding that the instances taken together were not arbitrary or capricious as a basis for discharge of a nonprobationary teacher.[26]

A Nebraska school guidance counselor was justifiably dismissed from his position for failing to register seniors in classes required for graduation and failing to inform parents of students who were having academic difficulties. The counselor had been specifically instructed to undertake these assignments, and lied to the school principal when asked if he was meeting the directives. The Nebraska Supreme Court affirmed the school board's decision to dismiss the counselor, holding that the counselor's disregard of the orders of the principal was neglect of duty and the counselor's untruthful statements to his superior constituted unprofessional conduct.[27]

A faculty member's failure to provide adequate supervision of students can serve as a basis for dismissal. In a case from Wyoming, a member of the music department faculty was notified of charges and provided with a hearing at which he was terminated for allowing students to drink alcohol and smoke marijuana on a sponsored trip. The reviewing state court denied an appeal based upon an alleged violation of due process of law, and ruled that the faculty member had a contractual obligation to provide supervision in the context of the sponsored trip and his failure to provide that supervision was sufficient to justify dismissal.[28]

INSUBORDINATION

Insubordination generally means a willful disregard of reasonable directives or a defiant attitude of noncompliance toward regulations specifically applicable to the employee. Dismissal on grounds of insubordination would be warranted for willful failures to follow directives that are reasonable, rationally related to the institution's educa-

---

[25]Bates v. Sponberg, 547 F. 2d 325 (6th Cir. 1976).
[26]Moffit v. Batesville School Dist., 643 S.W. 2d 557 (Ark. 1982).
[27]Bickford v. Board of Educ., 336 N.D. 2d 73 (Neb. 1983).
[28]White v. Board of Trustees of Western Wyoming Community College, 648 P. 2d 528 (Wyo. 1982).

tional objectives, and unambiguous. To justify dismissal, disobeying a directive must be shown to adversely impact the pursuit of educational goals or mission of the institution. This standard for insubordination will prevent unbridled discretion in using the violation of virtually any directive as a ground for dismissal. Under the detrimental effect test, charges of insubordination would not limit desirable, constructive dialogue within an institution nor deny a faculty or staff member's right to freedom of speech or academic freedom.

Courts have consistently affirmed administrative decisions to terminate the employment of faculty who refuse to comply with reasonable institutional policy or administrative directives. Instances of insubordination justifying termination have included the refusal of faculty to perform required professional duties as a form of protest over revision of institutional tenure policies,[29] taking of an unauthorized leave against the express direction of a university dean,[30] and persistent criticisms amounting to "verbal attacks" by faculty against administrators at the institution.[31] Dismissal for insubordination has also been justified upon evidence that the employee refused assignments,[32] or reacted in an argumentative, verbally hostile, and abusive fashion when directed to meet job requirements.[33]

Persistent acts of misconduct having a detrimental effect on institutional operation would justify dismissal for insubordination. Following several reprimands for being absent from the institution on numerous occasions, a tenured faculty member chose to ignore a directive denying a leave of absence and was absent at the beginning of the semester while delivering a paper at a conference in Israel. Dismissed for insubordination, the professor challenged on the grounds that his conduct was an exercise of an academic freedom privilege. The court rejected this contention, finding for the institution on the validity of the dismissal and concluding that the penalty of dismissal was not excessive when viewed in the context of a history of absenteeism.[34]

Repeated refusal to teach an assigned course would serve as a basis for dismissal on grounds of insubordination. A first refusal would not constitute repeated instances of a failure to obey a reasonable directive, but could serve as a basis for a reprimand or memo to the

[29]Shaw v. Board of Trustees, 549 *F.* 2d 929 (4th Cir. 1976).

[30]Stastny v. Board of Trustees Central Washington University, 647 *P.* 2d 496 (Wash. App. 1982), *cert. denied* 103 *S.Ct.* 1528 (1983).

[31]Roseman v. Indiana University of Pennsylvania, 520 *F.* 2d 1364 (3rd Cir. 1975), *cert. denied*, 424 *U.S.* 921 (1976).

[32]Alderstein v. Board of Educ., 485 *N.Y.S.* 2d 1 (App. Div. 1984); Board of Trustees v. Colwell, 611 *P.* 2d 427 (Wyo. 1980); and Booher v. Hogans, 468 *F. Supp.* 28 (E.D. Tenn. 1978).

[33]Clairton School Dist. v. Strinich, 413 *A.* 2d 26 (Pa. Commw. 1980).

[34]Stastny v. Board of Trustees of Central Washington University, 647 *P.* 2d 496 (Wash. App. 1982), *cert. denied*, 103 *S. Ct.* 1528 (1983).

employee file citing a specific instance of misconduct.[35] A tenured faculty member who initially refused to teach an assigned course received a contract stating that if he failed to accept the assignment in a second year he would be dismissed. The second refusal led to a hearing at which the faculty member was terminated for insubordination. Finding no violation of due process in the institution's hearing procedures, the reviewing federal court affirmed dismissal.[36]

A contention that a particular duty is not an express requirement and cannot be compelled is subject to a rule of reasonableness. In *Garrett v. Mathews*,[37] a federal court agreed that a faculty member's failure to comply with a reasonable request of a superior to supply a list of publications and to open mail from his superior constituted dereliction of duty and insubordination. The court observed: "Though, as plaintiff alleges, supplying a list of publications and opening mail may be nowhere written as job requirements, the court notes that not showing up for class naked is not a written job requirement either. Some things go without saying."[38]

Where institutional requirements are reasonable, and accompanied by adequate notice, they are enforceable. Two tenured medical faculty were dismissed for failure to comply with a university policy requiring faculty to sign agreements limiting outside income from medical practice. In a review of the dismissal, a federal appeals court recognized the authority of the institution to enforce limits on the amount of outside work a faculty member can undertake, violations of which would justify terminations.[39]

Insubordination charges often involve free speech or academic freedom defenses asserted by employees. In *Hillis v. Stephen F. Austin State University*,[40] a nontenured faculty member who was denied contract renewal challenged his department chair's characterization of his work performance as "insubordinate" and alleged he was not rehired because of his exercise of free speech. The Fifth Circuit Court of Appeals reversed a lower court decision favoring the nonrenewed art teacher and found sufficient evidence on the record to establish that the probationary, annual contract employee was not renewed for reasons unrelated to free speech.[41] Specifically, the court found that there was testimony from university officials that the faculty member was loud, abusive, and insubordinate on several occasions prior to the decision to terminate his employment.[42] This testimony included accounts of "yelling" at a female employee who was explaining a policy

[35]Adams v. Lake City Community College, 404 So. 2d 148 (Fla. App. 1981).
[36]Smith v. Kent State Univ., 696 F. 2d 476 (6th Cir. 1983).
[37]474 F. Supp. 594 (N.D. Ala. 1979), aff'd 625 F. 2d 658 (5th Cir. 1980).
[38]Id. at 599.
[39]448 F. Supp. 245 (W.D. Tenn. 1978).
[40]665 F. 2d 547 (5th Cir. 1982).
[41]Id. at 552
[42]Id. 551

and use of improper language and other general rudeness. In addition, the court identified a specific instance of insubordination in which the faculty member had refused to assign a grade for a student in his graduate art class after being directed to do so by the department chairman.[43]

In *Keddie* v. *Pennsylvania State University*,[44] a federal district court enumerated several legitimate institutional interests that would limit the public university faculty member's right to say and do as he or she pleased. These institutional interests would include:

1. Insure discipline and harmony among co-workers;
2. Permit confidentiality;
3. Limit conduct which impedes proper performance of daily duties;
4. Encourage loyalty and confidence among employees and superiors;
5. Allow divergent views (or limit proselytizing in the classroom);
6. Provide orderly functioning of the university.[45]

Courts must balance the interest of the employee in commenting on matters of public concern against the institution's interest in maintaining the efficiency of the educational program. In *Shaw* v. *Board of Trustees of Frederick Community College*,[46] two professors, one tenured and one on a continuing appointment, were dismissed for boycotting a faculty workshop and commencement exercises in protest of plans to prospectively abolish tenure at the college. The court held that the First Amendment did not give them the right to violate the terms of their employment.[47]

In decisions affirming the evidentiary sufficiency of contract cancellations under Alabama law, public school teachers were found insubordinate for refusal to follow rules established by a department head,[48] refusal to attend an enrichment program,[49] and refusal to obey a guidance counselor's reasonable request to return to the classroom.[50]

Facts giving rise to a dismissal for insubordination were reviewed in a Supreme Court of Mississippi decision upholding a board's termination of a teaching contract. The record indicated that the teacher had repeatedly refused to sign an attachment to all district teaching contracts which had been proposed by the superintendent and approved by the board. After requesting on several occasions that the

---

[43]*Id.* at 552-553.

[44]412 *F. Supp.* 1264 (M.D. Pa. 1976).

[45]*Id.* at 1271.

[46]549 F. 2d 929 (4th Cir. 1976).

[47]*Id.* at 932.

[48]Aaron v. Alabama State Tenure Comm'n, 407 *So.* 2d 136 (Ala. Civ. App. 1981).

[49]Howell v. Alabama Tenure Comm'n, 402 *So.* 2d 1041 (Ala. Civ. App. 1981).

[50]Heath v. Alabama State Tenure Comm'n, 401 *So.* 2d 68 (Ala. Civ. App. 1981), *cert. denied*, Ex parte Heath, 401 *So.* 2d 72 (Ala. 1981).

teacher sign the attachment, the superintendent wrote the teacher a letter telling her that if she did not sign within a given period of time he would recommend that she be dismissed for insubordination. The record disclosed other uncooperative behavior on the part of the teacher, but the high court concluded that even if the refusal to sign the attachment had been the sole reason for discharge it would have been sufficient.[51]

In a case in Pennsylvania involving termination for negligence and persistent and willful violation of school laws, the tenured teacher sought to overturn the school board's dismissal decision by arguing a right to academic and religious freedom. The elementary school teacher had regularly undertaken religious exercises in his classroom, including Bible reading and audible prayer. Although state statutes permitted a period of silent meditation, the Bible reading and extemporaneous prayer violated the First Amendment's establishment clause and was not authorized by state law. The teacher's refusal to comply with the superintendent's directives to cease the religious exercises was held to be a valid cause for termination.[52]

Insubordination is often defined as the continuing and willful refusal to obey a superior's reasonable orders. Following unsatisfactory ratings of classroom performance, an Arizona teacher was instructed to meet with the school principal on a daily basis for the purpose of reviewing lesson plans and upgrading performance. The teacher refused to attend these sessions after sixteen meetings on the grounds that they were unproductive and designed merely as a scheme to support his dismissal. The school board's dismissal of the teacher was upheld on the basis that his continuing refusal to attend the meetings was insubordinate.[53]

A science teacher with nineteen years' experience was dismissed for insubordination under Mississippi statute law following several incidents in which he refused assignments involving supervision of students at a football game and during examinations on school grounds. The teacher contended it was error for the board to consider testimony as to the first instance of insubordination since it had never become a record in his personnel file and had taken place a year previous to the second instance. The Supreme Court of Mississippi held otherwise, noting that the admission in evidence of both instances was justified to establish a "constant or continuing intentional refusal to obey a direct or implied order."[54]

Dismissal for insubordination would not be permissible under circumstances in which the employee's refusal to perform as ordered was

[51]Sims v. Board of Trustees of Holly Springs, 414 *So.* 2d 431 (Miss. 1982).
[52]Fink v. Board of Educ. of Warren, 442 *A.* 2d 837 (Pa. Commw. 1982).
[53]Siglin v. Kayenta Unified School Dist., 655 *P.* 2d 353 (Ariz. App. 1982).
[54]Jackson v. Hazlehurst Mun. Separate School Dist., 427 *So.* 2d 134 (Miss. 1983).

reasonable. When a superior sought to compel a community college employee to sign an inculpatory statement under threat of dismissal for insubordination, the employee's refusal to sign was not insubordination justifying dismissal. The reviewing court concluded the employee could properly refuse to sign such a statement, which, had it been signed, would have made an administrative hearing on charges of misconduct irrelevant.[55]

IMMORAL OR UNETHICAL CONDUCT

Judicial decisions do not provide a precise definition of immorality in the context of higher education. Rather than establish a single standard, immorality encompasses conduct that offends contemporary moral standards, is inconsistent with moral rectitude, or evokes condemnation by the academic community.

In cases involving cause for dismissal based on immoral conduct, the detrimental effect test balances the institution's need for adequate authority to remove faculty and staff whose conduct harms the educational process, while it honors the individual's freedom to conduct his or her personal life as he or she chooses. The test recognizes that the employee's private conduct is a proper concern to the institution only to the extent that the conduct reflects on the employee's ability to perform in the educational setting

The employee's ability to perform is a proper focus of inquiry in judging fitness relative to a charge of immorality. If a faculty member's allegedly immoral conduct seriously undermines the respect he or she gains from students or colleagues, a finding of unfitness could be justified. This might occur if students observe a faculty member's public sexual behavior or if publicity calls attention to a teacher's arrest on criminal charges. Even in these cases, however, the effect of notoriety should be examined realistically to determine whether its long-range consequences warrant dismissing an otherwise capable educator.

Reviewing courts will often assume that public knowledge of a faculty or staff member's misconduct will negate whatever goodwill and respect he or she has earned through years of employment. However, the employee may be able to restore confidence among students and colleagues promptly so that the educational process is not impaired, and in some instances it would be reasonable for an administrative board to allow a brief period of time for this restoration to take place.

In *Morrison* v. *State Board of Education*,[56] a public school teacher had admitted engaging in a noncriminal homosexual relationship. The

---

[55]Smith v. Gwydin, 446 *N.Y.S.* 2d 385 (App. Div. 1982).
[56]461 *P.* 2d 375 (Cal. 1969).

24

California State Board of Education found that the teacher's behavior, which was characterized as "immoral," justified permanent revocation of the teaching certificate. No evidence was presented, however, indicating an impairment of his ability to teach or diminution in his educational effectiveness. The California Supreme Court analogized its decisions on bar admission and disciplinary proceedings for attorneys and license revocation decisions by a board of examiners for doctors to the issue of teacher fitness.[57] Under these circumstances, revocation, disbarment, or denial of admission was found permissible only when the acts in question could be shown to directly bear on the individual's fitness to practice. The court concluded that any factors considered in a decision to dismiss a tenured teacher were relevant only to the "extent that they assist the board in determining . . . whether the teacher's future classroom performance and overall impact on his students are likely to meet the board's standards."[58] In holding for the teacher, the court emphasized the lack of evidence of any classroom ineffectiveness to support the standard of substantial evidence for revocation of certificate.[59]

The decision in *Morrison* emphasized that a direct impairment of teaching ability or an adverse effect on the institution's operation must be shown. In a Florida case, *Texton* v. *Hancock*,[60] a tenured professor was dismissed for immorality, misconduct in office, and willful neglect of duty. The professor was accused of using profanity and sexual references in class, drinking heavily at a student's home, asking a student to have an affair with her ex-husband, and other acts of misbehavior. The Florida appeals court observed that "if a school teacher is responsible for teaching students in their formative years and commits acts of immorality after school hours, such acts may be indirectly related to misconduct in office," but that "Ms. Texton's conduct must be judged in the context of her more liberal, open, robust college surroundings."[61] The court held that the evidence amounted merely to "indiscretions" by the plaintiff and could not constitute sufficient grounds for dismissal when viewed in the context of a higher education institution.[62]

Among the types of behavior which are most frequently associated with immorality or moral turpitude, courts have acknowledged conviction of a crime, sexual misconduct, dishonesty and ribald or vulgar behavior. Charges of immorality based upon sexual misconduct which is of an open and notorious nature have served as a proper basis of

---

[57]*Id.* at 379-382.
[58]*Id.* at 387.
[59]*Id.* at 391-393.
[60]359 *So.* 2d 895 (Fla. App. 1978).
[61]*Id.* at 897.
[62]*Id.* at 896.

dismissal even absent a showing of a direct detrimental effect,[63] however, a failure to show that the allegedly immoral conduct seriously undermines job performance has resulted in some decisions overruling dismissal on this ground.[64] Criminal arrest and conviction, and in some instances arrest with adjudication of guilt withheld, would warrant dismissal for immorality where the seriousness of the charge and the adverse publicity surrounding the case could reasonably be predicted to have a direct detrimental effect.[65]

Notoriety can often create a presumption of detrimental effect. A California community college faculty member was discovered by a deputy sheriff while parked at night in an unlit industrial area near the college. The faculty member and a student in one of his classes were observed, partially undressed, in the front seat of the car. The sheriff was forced to engage in an auto chase when the faculty member first threatened the officer and then sought to drive away. In noting that responsible conduct at the college level would not include a meretricious relationship with students and assaults on police officers in the presence of a student, the state court affirmed dismissal for immoral conduct.[66] While no direct evidence of lack of fitness was present in the record, the court noted that the potential for notoriety associated with the faculty member's lack of discretion in choosing a parking location proximate to the campus, coupled with his verbal assault and attempted escape from the sheriff, ultimately assured the level of notoriety which would be presumed to affect teaching fitness.[67]

Sexual harassment, whether aimed at students or colleagues, also constitutes adequate cause for dismissal. A tenured professor charged with sexual harassment of several female students was provided a hearing before a specially created faculty committee designed to hear such complaints. After the hearing, the committee concluded cause for dismissal existed and recommended termination. Although a separate faculty panel had been established to hear faculty employment issues, the governing board did not refer this matter to that panel, and dismissed the professor consistent with the recommendation of the committee designed to review allegations of harassment. The Fifth Circuit Court of Appeals found that the decision to dismiss was proper and held that no violation of constitutional due process resulted from the review by the specially created faculty committee.[68] The nature and significance of the allegations, coupled with substantial com-

---

[63]See Thompson v. Southwest School Dist., 483 F. Supp. 1170 (W.D. Mo 1980).

[64]See Sherburne v. School Bd. of Suwannee, 455 So. 2d 1057 (Fla. App. 1984).

[65]See Dowing v. Mays, 257 S.F. 2d 317 (Ga. App. 1979) (arrest for possession of illegal drugs) and Gillett v. Unified School Dist., 605 P. 2d 105 (Kan. 1980) (shoplifting).

[66]Board of Trustees of Compton College v. Stubblefield, 94 Cal. Rptr. 318 (Cal. App. 1971).

[67]Id. at 322.

[68]Levitt v. University of Texas at El Paso, 759 F. 2d 1224 (5th Cir. 1985).

pliance under standards of due process justified dismissal of the tenured faculty member.[69]

Misconduct involving charges of sexual harassment applies to both faculty and staff. The Supreme Court of Washington affirmed an academic council's dismissal of a tenured professor for sexual advances toward female students, faculty, and staff and the wives of faculty and staff.[70] The academic council concluded that this misconduct constituted behavior "reflecting seriously upon the college or upon the character and reputation of the person involved."[71] In a case from Oregon, a resident supervisor of a university's high school equivalency program was terminated for cause based upon charges of sexual harassment.[72] The court found that there was substantial evidence to support the charges in that the employee had conversed in sexual overtones with female students and one of the female resident assistants, berated an employee after she resisted his advances, and conducted evening room checks in women's dormitories after he had been instructed not to do so.[73]

A faculty or staff member's sexual contact with a student, particularly an undergraduate student or a student in the faculty member's classes, could serve as a basis for discipline or dismissal. In a public school case, the New York Commissioner of Education's decision that a teacher was unfit was supported by substantial evidence, and the penalty of dismissal was fair when the teacher admitted that he put his arm around and kissed female students, improperly touched students by giving them a "pat on the behind," and permitted obscene jokes and profanity in his classroom.[74] A female instructor, reassigned rather than dismissed for having an intimate relationship with a female undergraduate who was not in her classes, challenged the reassignment was discrimination based upon sexual orientation. The Fifth Circuit Court of Appeals affirmed the reassignment, adopting the institution's contention that any intimate relationship between a faculty member and a student at the institution, whether homosexual or heterosexual, constituted unprofessional conduct.[75]

A tenured professor, arrested for making and soliciting lewd and indecent acts on the university campus, admitted soliciting lewd acts in the student union restrooms although he was not formally charged with a crime. Following an investigation by two separate university committees, hearings were held and the professor's employment was

[69]Id.
[70]Lehman v. Board of Trustees of Whitman College, 576 P. 2d 397 (Wash. 1978).
[71]Id. at 399.
[72]Loera v. State Bd. of Higher Educ., 609 P. 2d 826 (Or. App. 1980).
[73]Id. at 829.
[74]Katz v. Ambach, 472 N.Y.S. 2d 757 (App. Div. 1984).
[75]Naragon v. Wharton, 572 F. Supp. 1117 (M.D. La. 1983).

reviewed. Neither committee recommended dismissal for acts involving moral turpitude, but the university governing board rejected probation and acted to dismiss on the basis of the facts established in the investigation and subsequent hearings. finding no violation of procedural due process, a federal appeals court affirmed dismissal, finding that the issue was not whether the professor's acts affected his teaching but whether the nature of his acts constituted moral turpitude.[76]

Criminal misconduct, particularly where a matter of public notoriety, can serve as a grounds for dismissal. A teacher's possession of marijuana was held to be irremediable conduct, not requiring a warning and an opportunity to correct, in a case from Illinois involving dismissal for cause. Following arrest and a plea of guilty to charges of possession, the teacher was dismissed for immorality. In determining whether a detrimental effect resulted from the teacher's conduct, the court said:

> We are aware of the special position occupied by a teacher in our society. As a consequence of that elevated stature, a teacher's actions are subject to much greater scrutiny than that given to the activities of the average person. We do not doubt that knowledge of a teacher's involvement in illegalities such as possession of marijuana would have a major deleterious effect upon the school system and would greatly impede that individual's ability to adequately fulfill his role.[77]

In an unusual administrative law case from New York, a teacher who was officially reprimanded by the school board for misconduct sought to overturn the board's decision as an excessive penalty. The appellate court took note that the reprimand was related to conviction for the felonious offense of drug possession and concluded that the reprimand was not excessive; rather, it was so lenient as to be arbitrary and capricious and an abuse of the board's discretion. The court ordered the board to reconsider its decision, presumably to enforce dismissal as the appropriate penalty.[78]

A faculty member who pleaded guilty to grand theft for improper billing to a medical provider was required to repay $5,431.50 to the provider and pay a $1,000.00 fine. The conviction led the president of the institution to initiate charges of immorality based upon conviction of a crime involving moral turpitude. Despite a faculty committee finding of no evidence of immoral conduct justifying dismissal, the university president's decision to dismiss was upheld by a California appeals court on the basis that the faculty member's honesty had been significantly impugned and the penalty of dismissal was not an abuse

---

[76]Corstvet v. Borger, 757 F. 2d 223 (10th Cir. 1985).
[77]Chicago Bd. of Educ. v. Payne, 430 N.E. 2d 310, 315 (Ill. 1981).
[78]Riforgiato v. Board of Educ., 448 N.Y.S. 2d 74 (App. Div. 1982).

of discretion.[79] Although the faculty committee found no evidence of nexus between the faculty member's impropriety and his fitness to teach, the appeals court did not consider *direct* evidence of a detrimental effect a critical variable.[80]

A tenured public high school teacher, convicted of diverting electricity from an electric cooperative by using a splice line that bypassed a residential meter was sentenced to a jail term and required to make restitution. His school district board provided notice and hearing, then moved to dismiss for a crime involving moral turpitude. The teacher's dismissal for moral turpitude was justified by the board on the basis of his conviction for willfully diverting electricity, which the board considered a form of larceny or theft. The teacher argued that the concept of "moral turpitude" was too vague and, alternatively, that the board failed to show any relationship between his conviction and a direct detrimental affect on classroom performance. In affirming the board's dismissal decision, the Supreme Court of Alaska noted that it was reasonable to assume that the conviction was for a crime involving moral turpitude, and concluded that no "classroom nexus" between the behavior and classroom effectiveness need be shown where criminal conviction served as the basis for a proof of moral turpitude justifying dismissal.[81]

In instances in which the institution could be liable for faculty misconduct, institutional agents have an affirmative duty to monitor faculty performance and review allegations of unprofessional conduct. Substantial evidence of sexual harassment violative of the provisions of Title VII (governing employment) or Title IX (governing students or other beneficiaries of programs receiving federal financial assistance) could justify dismissal for immoral conduct.[82] Similarly, violations of research protocols under federal statutes or regulations,[83] falsification of data, plagiarism, abuse of confidentiality or other unethical conduct could constitute violations of scientific or scholarly practice justifying dismissal for cause.[84]

A faculty member, terminated for misrepresenting his academic credentials, alleged that his misrepresentations were not relevant to his job performance and could not be used as a proper basis for dismissal. Although there was evidence the faculty member had performed

---

[79]Samaan v. Trustees of the California State University and Colleges, 197 *Cal. Rptr.* 856 (Cal. App. 1983).

[80]*Id.* at 859, note 59.

[81]Kenai Peninsula Borough Bd. of Educ. v. Brown, 691 *P.* 2d 1034 (Alaska 1984).

[82]*See* 42 *U.S.C.* 2000(d) (1976) and 20 *U.S.C.* 1681 (1976).

[83]*See* Human Subjects Research, 45 *C.F.R.* 46.101-.409 (1983), Guidelines for Research Involving Recombinant DNA Molecules, 48 *Fed. Reg.* 24556 (1983) and The Animal Welfare Act of 1970, 7 *U.S.C.* 2131 (1982).

[84]*See* Olswang and Lee, "Scientific Misconduct: Institutional Procedures and Due Process Considerations," 11 *J. of C. and Univ. L.*, 51-64 (1984).

duties satisfactorily, he had disclosed he held no academic degree to an administrative superior. In upholding the termination for cause, and denying the former employee's claim for unemployment compensation, a California appeals court ruled that academic degree requirements are clearly relevant to a faculty position and would have adversely affected the college if discovered by accrediting agencies.[85]

A professor who claimed when he was hired that he would obtain a master's degree within a few months, but did not do so, was granted tenure three years later, accepted the salary of a faculty member with a masters degree, and wore a master's gown to graduation ceremonies. When the truth was discovered, the tenured professor was terminated. The federal district court affirmed, recognizing dishonesty in the faculty member's misrepresentation as a valid basis for dismissal.[86]

Failure of a college faculty member to provide evidence of his scholarly degrees and refusal to sign release forms which would authorize the university to obtain documentation of degrees led to an administrative hearing finding just cause for dismissal. In upholding the administrative board, an Illinois appellate court found the board's decision supported by substantial evidence and affirmed the position that an institution's inquiry into a faculty member's academic credentials is not shielded by a right to privacy and is within the institution's legitimate and reasonable concerns.[87]

A tenured public school professional employee who filed a report of excused absence due to illness was dismissed by the school board when later events established that she had misrepresented her reason for absence in order to attend a professional conference. Although the Pennsylvania Commissioner of Education rejected good cause termination based on the ground of immorality, the state appellate court reversed, upholding the authority of the board to determine what constitutes "immorality" upon consideration of appropriate professional standards and the sufficiency of evidence.[88]

Encouraging student dishonesty would certainly justify dismissal. A public school wrestling coach who encouraged his athletes to cheat by wrestling outside their weight and class was dismissed for immoral conduct and lack of teaching fitness. The federal district court affirmed dismissal, noting that the dishonesty would certainly have a direct detrimental effect upon the students involved in the wrestling program.[89]

[85]Denberg v. Foretto Heights College, 694 P. 2d 375 (Colo. App. 1985).
[86]Barszez v. Board of Trustees, 400 F. Supp. 675 (N.D. Ill. 1975).
[87]Karayanakis v. State Universities Civil Service Merit Board, 474 N.E. 2d 938 (Ill. App. 1985).
[88]Bethel Park School Dist. v. Krall, 445 A. 2d 1377 (Pa. Commw. Ct. 1982).
[89]Florian v. Highland Local School Dist., 570 F. Supp. 1358 (D. Ohio 1983).

Chapter III

Legal Challenges to Adequate Cause for Dismissal

In general, an employee who is dismissed may challenge the governing board's adverse employment decision by an appeal to a state or federal court. This appeal is normally considered to be limited to the function of determining the legality, and not the propriety, of the governing board's decisions. Matters over which a court is likely to intervene would normally include violations of constitutional or statutory provisions, decisions made upon unsupported or insubstantial evidence and decisions which are arbitrary or capricious or otherwise characterized by abuse of discretion.

The level of scrutiny employed by the courts in reviewing the governing board's action will vary. If a violation of First or Fourteenth Amendment constitutional guarantees is established by the employee, the court may adopt a strict scrutiny standard, requiring the public institution's governing board to show a compelling interest for the challenged action. In other instances, as where a dismissal for incompetency is predicated on evidence of unsatisfactory classroom performance, courts have avoided applying a rigorous evidentiary standard, requiring only that the governing board's action be supported by substantial evidence and that the policy on dismissal be reasonably related to a valid institutional purpose.

In these latter instances, where there is evidence to support the board's findings, and where the cause for dismissal found by the board can reasonably be said to relate to the efficient operation of the institution, the reviewing court will normally limit its examination to whether the board has proceeded within the limits of its jurisdiction, whether adequate due process was provided, and whether there was any prejudicial abuse of discretion.

BASIC ADMONITIONS

A review of case law focused on challenges to the policies or practices utilized by institutions to justify dismissal decisions yields three basic admonitions critical to the development and implementation of employment practices related to dismissal for cause. First, adequate cause standards must be reasonably related to job requirements and professional fitness. Second, employment practices should yield substantial, relevant and credible evidence to justify an adverse employment decision uncompromised by considerations that are unrelated to professional performance. Third, procedures which guide employment practices should be clearly articulated, publicized, and properly followed.

Adoption of job-related adequate cause standards should be a high priority in the development of policy. Standards must conform to state statutory mandates, state and local board regulation, and negotiated agreement. Where appropriate, state certification requirements, professional training, years of previous experience, degree requirements, and other objective indices should be expressly stated in the adopted standards. However, job-relatedness should be the principal consideration in adopting standards and the institution must be prepared to articulate the relationship between a particular standard and job-performance which will avoid a challenge of vagueness or irrelevance.

Standards utilized in assessing faculty or staff performance may include both objective and subjective factors. What is critical is not whether subjective judgments are made and ultimately relied upon, but whether the standards on which judgments are predicated were validly related to the requirements of the position, observable, and properly applied. While employment decisions based upon subjective criteria are likely to be closely scrutinized by courts because of the potential for masking unlawful bias, evidence that the standards are job-related will permit an inference of reasonableness.

The faculty member's ability to work cooperatively with professional colleagues and provide proper instruction or supervision are valid considerations in evaluating performance. Periodic performance reviews, anecdotal records and reports of student and faculty evaluations can be utilized to support unsatisfactory performance appraisals. While the cumulative weight of evidence justifying an adverse employment decision may be subject to a court's determination of how substantial the evidence of adequate cause may be, it is clear that courts are deferential to administrative decisions predicated on reasonable standards of performance.

A tenured faculty member and former department chair with a history of unexcused absences from classes and faculty meetings, undocumented research, and student complaints of poor teaching performance was terminated after reviews by a committee of the faculty senate and the regents of the university. The review panels relied upon testimony from faculty and the department chair and on a documentary record of annual merit evaluations and student complaints which supported charges of unsatisfactory performance. In affirming termination, the reviewing federal appeals court found no violation of due process or evidence of discrimination in the dismissal, and noted that it was not the role of the court to review the evidentiary record to assess whether the court agreed with termination as this determination was within the authority of the regents.[1]

Evidence that a faculty member was a disruptive rather than contributive influence, refused to follow reasonable directives, and was unwilling to observe rules and regulations has been upheld as a justification for unsatisfactory evaluations leading to nonrenewal.[2] While "failure to work with the administration" may not be sufficient to justify nonrenewal,[3] difficulty in working with faculty colleagues is often presumed by courts to implicate ineffective performance and is a judicially recognized factor which would justify an unsatisfactory performance evaluation having adverse consequences for the employee.[4] Similarly, abusive and arbitrary treatment of students, ineffective use of instructional materials, harassment, and related classroom improprieties have been judicially accepted indicia of unsatisfactory performance.[5]

The institution's employment practices must reflect fundamental fairness and reasonableness in application to faculty and professional staff, and yield a documentary record substantial enough, as to cumulative evidentiary weight, to justify the dismissal decision. While evidence need not always be characterized as objective, it must be relevant, credible and substantial. Educational institutions, as one court has noted, are not "married to mediocrity, but may dismiss personnel who are neither performing high quality work nor improving in performance."[6] Nevertheless, unsubstantiated claims of inadequate performance, conflicting appraisals of performance or lack of a uniform standard in the evaluation and documentation process may contribute to the view that the institution lacks sufficient basis for any adverse employment decision.

Although subjective evaluation is involved, judicial opinions have sustained the use of peer and supervisory evaluations in employment

[1]King v. University of Minnesota, 774 F. 2d 224 (8th Cir. 1985).
[2]Sharnhorst v. Independent School Dist., 686 F. 2d 637 (8th Cir. 1982).
[3]See Haddock v. Board of Educ., 661 P. 2d 368 (Kan. 1983).
[4]See Grant v. Board of Educ. of School Dirs. of Centennial, 417 A. 2d 1292 (Pa. Commw. 1984) and Yielding v. Crockett Independent School Dist., 707 F. 2d 196 (5th Cir. 1983).
[5]See Donnes v. State, 672 P. 2d 617 (Mont. 1983) (abusive and arbitrary with students); Carson City School Dist. v. Burnsen, 608 P. 2d 507 (Neb. 1980) (poor lesson planning and ineffective use of materials); and Fay v. Board of Dirs. of North-Linn, 298 N.W. 2d 345 (Iowa App. 1980) (harassment of students and lack of rapport with students).
[6]Briggs v. Board of Dirs., 282 N.W. 2d 740, at 743 (Iowa 1979).

decision-making. Court reliance upon observation reports completed by supervisors and persons knowledgeable in a teacher's subject matter field illustrates the considerable weight given to the evidentiary value of these records.[7] Evaluation reports by different faculty or staff would reduce bias and substantiate unsatisfactory performance when reports are corroborative. Specification of deficiencies, consistent with recognized, job-related standards, together with reasonable opportunities for remediation and periodic reevaluation supports the fundamental fairness of the review or evaluation process. Post-observation conferences, in which deficiencies are detailed and suggestions for remediation are offered, strengthens the view that the evaluation process is fair. Other forms of documentation, such as anecdotal records and formal reports of complaints or reprimands, contribute to the overall evidentiary weight to be accorded unsatisfactory performance evaluations.[8] Follow-up evaluations which indicate the faculty member has made no progress within a reasonable time period for remediation or which establish that the faculty member either disregarded remediation or regarded remediation lightly would confirm the appropriateness of the adverse employment decision.[9]

The failure to effectuate evaluation processes which yield relevant, credible and substantial evidence to support employment decisions may lead to a system which fails to justify employment decisions and ultimately utilizes announced evaluation processes as a subterfuge for unlawful employment practices. This system may be manipulated such that employment decisions are predicated upon superficial or unrelated aspects of job performance or job requirements. Under these circumstances, a court might conclude the employer fashioned a house of straw, which was unable to withstand the fresh breeze of judicial scrutiny.[10]

The institution's adoption and implementation of procedures to guide employment practices can serve to establish fundamental ele-

---

[7]*See,* for example, Thompson v. School Dist. of Omaha, 623 F. 2d 46 (8th Cir. 1980) (evaluations by math instructor and co-worker confirmed unsatisfactory performance evaluation by principal).

[8]*See,* for example, Patterson v. Masem, 594 F. *Supp.* 386 (E.D. Ark. 1984) (school district established basis for denying black applicant supervisory position on basis of negative performance evaluations coupled with corroborating testimony of co-workers and specific incident memorandum) and Davison v. Winston-Salem-Forsyth County Bd. of Educ., 303 *S.E.* 2d 202 (N.C. App. 1983) (principal's evaluations coupled with record of parental complaints of poor teaching justified dismissal).

[9]*See* Thompson v. Board of Educ., 668 *P.* 2d 954 (Colo. App. 1983) (failure to follow principal's reasonable suggestions for improved teaching performance appropriately a ground for dismissal for insubordination); Siglin v. Kayenta Unified School Dist., 655 *P.* 2d 353 (Ariz. App. 1982) (insubordination dismissal upheld for refusal to attend daily lesson plan reviews); and Board of Dirs. of Sioux City Community School Dist. v. Mroz, 295 *N.W.* 2d 447 (Iowa 1980) (termination for incompetency after failure to cooperate in efforts to improve performance).

[10]*See* Hollingsworth v. Board of Educ., 303 *N.W.* 2d 506 (Neb. 1984).

ments of due process of law. For public higher education institutions, provisions of appropriate due process are uniquely a function of the particular state's laws harmonized with the guarantees of the Fourteenth Amendment. Employment procedures utilized within a college or university can elaborate the elements of due process that would insure compliance with delineated standards. In one case, a court's examination of institutional evaluation procedures led to a judicial determination that the employee had been accorded all the necessary elements of due process protection before dismissal. Among the evaluation procedures provided, the court specifically emphasized notice and specification of evaluation standards in advance of evaluation, availability of evaluation reports, opportunity to review and respond to evaluations, reasonable time to correct deficiencies prior to a second evaluation, and notice and an opportunity to contest employment decisions on which evaluations would be based.[11]

Among public institutions, the degree of procedural protections available to the employee vary with the particular state's recognition of a property right in employment or a liberty interest in preserving other employment opportunities.[12] However, courts have been relatively uniform in requiring notice of the standards to be utilized in evaluating employee performance and institutional conformance with procedures for informing the employee of deficiencies in performance. Courts also require evidence that the institution complied substantially with the statutory or regulatory provisions governing procedural due process. A probationary teacher in West Virginia won reinstatement when she established that she was neither openly evaluated, nor given a meaningful opportunity to learn what deficiencies were identified in order that she might correct them.[13] Failure to provide a tenured teacher with a preliminary notice of alleged inadequacies in teaching performance resulted in her reinstatement under Arizona law.[14] In a similar case from Montana, a probationary teacher was reinstated to annual contract status when the court found the stated reason for nonrenewal was insufficient to advise the teacher of his deficiencies.[15]

An institution's failure to follow adopted procedures can be characterized as a lack of compliance with appropriate due process.[16]

---

[11]Needleman v. Bohlen, 602 F. 2d 1 (1st Cir. 1979).

[12]Compare, for example, Shatting v. Dillingham City School Dist., 617 P. 2d 9 (Alaska 1980) (nonrenewal may be based upon any reason considered adequate by the board) with Mason Cty. Bd. of Educ. v. State Superintendent, 274 S.E. 2d 435 (W. Va. 1980) (board failure to base dismissal upon evaluations *after* the employee is afforded an improvement period to correct conduct is arbitrary).

[13]Lipan v. Board of Education of Hancock, 295 S.E. 2d 44 (W. Va. 1982) *See also*, Wilt v. Flanigan, 294 S.E. 2d 189 (W. Va. 1982) (teacher reinstated when remediable deficiencies were not called to her attention through evaluation).

[14]Orth v. Phoenix Union High School System, 613 P. 2d 311 (Ariz. App. 1980).

[15]Bridger Educ. Ass'n v. Board of Trustees of Carbon County School Dist., 678 P. 2d 659 (Mont. 1984).

[16]*See* Nzomo v. Vermont State Colleges, 385 A. 2d 1099 (Vt. 1978).

However, failure to conform to every technical detail of an institution's termination procedures would not create a violation of procedural due process. Provisions of due process in faculty termination proceedings must be substantially followed, but strict adherence to the conditions of a faculty handbook or employment agreement will not be compelled if reasonable due process protections are provided to the aggrieved employee.[17]

The procedural safeguards afforded to employees at public institutions would not extend to the rigid formalities of a criminal prosecution, but would encompass certain procedural elements associated with judicial notions of fundamental fairness. Among these procedural elements, courts have required: (1) written notice of grounds for dismissal together with the allegations of misconduct related to those grounds; (2) opportunity for discovery of the evidence supporting the dismissal action; (3) opportunity to be heard and present witnesses at the hearing; (4) right to confront and cross-examine adverse witnesses; (5) impartial hearing by faculty peers; (6) a written statement by the hearing panel specifying the evidence which was relied upon in making the employment decision.[18]

Institutional compliance with substantive and procedural standards applicable to faculty/staff dismissal does not guarantee that litigation can be avoided, but compliance may reduce the incidence of successful legal challenges to dismissal decisions. Adoption and implementation of job-related performance standards, utilization of a documentation system that yields relevant and credible evidence of inadequate or improper performance, and adherence to procedural standards designed to provide fundamental fairness to the aggrieved employee can buttress the institution's position against legal challenge.

Four types of legal challenge are most common in cases involving dismissal for adequate cause. An understanding of the legal basis for these challenges should inform the employment decision making process. In the analysis that follows, the four principal legal challenges include denial of due process; denial of free speech, association or academic freedom; discrimination in employment and breach of contract.

DENIAL OF DUE PROCESS

Under the Fourteenth Amendment, an employee's interest in public employment may be constitutionally protected. Since procedural fairness must be observed whenever the disqualification of a public employee threatens his or her property or liberty interests, due process entitles the individual to notice of the reasons for the institution's

---

[17]See Piacitelli v. Southern Utah State College, 636 P. 2d 1063 (Utah 1981).
[18]See Chung v. Park, 514 F. 2d 382, 387 (3rd Cir. 1975).

action and an opportunity for a hearing on disputed issues of fact. These procedures are designed to mitigate official action which is arbitrary or capricious, but because a liberty or property interest must be established by the employee before any process becomes due, official action may be allowed to stand if a protectable interest is not found.

Liberty

A liberty interest may be infringed when the results of administrative action impose a stigma or other disability on the employee that forecloses the individual's freedom to take advantage of other employment opportunities, or otherwise injures good name, reputation or standing in the community. In *Board of Regents* v. *Roth*,[19] a faculty member hired to teach for one year at the university was informed, without explanation, that he would not be rehired. He alleged that the true reason for nonretention was his criticism of the university and insisted a due process hearing was required in which the university must justify its nonrenewal decision. The United States Supreme Court held that Roth failed to establish a violation of First Amendment free speech and no Fourteenth Amendment liberty interest was denied because the university had made no charges against Roth which would bar him from employment with another institution.[20]

In *Roth* no reasons were given for the professor's nonrenewal, but in *Beitzell* v. *Jeffrey*,[21] a faculty member who was denied tenure was unsuccessful in claiming the denial of a liberty interest even though his department chairman had submitted a memorandum to a grievance committee which described the professor's professional behavior as irresponsible and indicated that other faculty had expressed concern about the professor's drinking. The departmental committee had voted against a recommendation for tenure after a discussion which included references to the professor's lack of adequacy as a teacher and advisor and to his drinking. In all communications relevant to the decision not to grant tenure, the department chairman maintained a high level of confidentiality, disclosing the basis for the committee's decision to the professor and forwarding his memorandum to the grievance committee only when the professor's attorney insisted that the memo become a public record in the grievance proceedings. The appellate court observed that the professor failed to show that the personal aspects of these discussions, including references to drinking habits, became public as a result of the actions of the department chairman or the university.[22] Since the chairman did not make the charges public,

---

[19] 408 *U.S.* 564 (1972).
[20] *Id.* at 573.
[21] 643 *F.* 2d 870 (1st Cir. 1981).
[22] *Id.* at 875.

the university could not be said to have stigmatized the former employee in such a way as to interfere with his ability to take advantage of other employment opportunities.

The requirement that a stigma seriously damage the faculty member's ability to take advantage of other employment opportunities, coupled with the requirement of public disclosure of the reasons for the employment decision, has limited the number of cases in which faculty have successfully claimed a right to due process based on a denial of a liberty interest. An allegation of incompetence, standing alone, would be insufficient to support a charge that the employee's reputation had been so stigmatized as to compel due process of law.[23] A charge of inadequate teaching performance would appear to be insufficient to establish a stigma denying a liberty interest,[24] rather a showing that the institution made public charges that the employee had been guilty of unprofessional conduct or immorality would seem required.

Property

To compel due process protections, a public employee might show that a property interest exists which is sufficient to justify court intervention. Typically, whether a legitimate claim of entitlement to continued employment exists will be defined in reference to employee contracts, negotiated agreements, institutional regulations and state laws. Faculty in public institutions who are dismissed or otherwise denied property rights during the term of employment are entitled to due process of law. This view is consistent with the decision in *Perry* v. *Sindermann*,[25] in which the Supreme Court ruled that a teacher who had held his faculty position for four years, in reliance upon a *defacto* tenure arrangement, could establish a legitimate claim of entitlement worthy of due process protection. The Court cautioned, though, that "if it is the law (of the state) that a teacher . . . has no contractual or other claim to job tenure, the . . . claim would be defeated."[26]

The faculty member involved in the *Perry* case was able to establish *defacto* tenure by coupling the institution's lack of a formal tenure system with oral and written representations that satisfactory performance would be rewarded with continuing employment. Numerous appellate decisions have distinguished the *Perry* case by emphasizing that an established system with published standards and procedures for granting tenure would not allow for a *defacto* grant of tenure. Assurances of tenure given a faculty member by an institution's agents would not appear to create a sufficient expectation of con-

---

[23]Loehr v. Ventura County Community College, 743 F. 2d 1310 (9th Cir. 1984).
[24]Swain v. Board of Trustees, 466 F. *Supp.* 120 (N.D. Ohio 1979).
[25] 408 *U.S.* 593.
[26]*Id.* at 599.

tinued employment guaranteeing due process protections when the assurances are clearly contradicted by published tenure policies.[27] A promise by a department chair that a new professor would receive tenure "as a matter of course" or assurances by tenured colleagues that a professor is progressing satisfactorily and would eventually receive tenure would not create an implied right to tenure when the non-tenured faculty member is given notice of a formal tenure process.[28]

The extent of process which is due depends on a balancing of the public institution's interest in efficient operation of the system against the weight of the property or liberty interest of the individual. The seriousness and permanence of an adverse employment decision will influence the requirements for notice and/or hearing and the extent to which administrative appeal and review are necessary. Generally, where the faculty member has established a property or liberty interest worthy of due process, minimal elements afforded to the employee would include the following:

1. Notice of cause for termination in sufficient detail to fairly enable the employee to show any error that may exist;
2. Notice of the names of witnesses and the nature of their testimony as it relates to the cause for termination;
3. Hearing within a reasonable period of time at which the employee may respond to allegations;
4. Impartial hearing panel possessed of a reasonable level of expertise relative to the charges.[29]

An institution's formal grievance procedure established for administrative review of employment decisions should accord the minimal elements of due process. A specific agent of the institution must be charged with the responsibility of providing notice to the employee, informing the employee of the charges, procedures and consequences of any action which might be taken and outlining the route of appeal. Failure to provide timely notice to the employee has resulted in a court-ordered continuation of employment, specifically when the college or university has promulgated rules on notice of non-renewal and the agent of the institution fails to notify within the period established for the notice of non-retention.[30] Similarly, a department chairman's failure to discuss his renewal recommendations with a non-tenured faculty member, when college procedural rules specifically required such notice, has resulted in continuation of employment for the affected employee.[31] Both these results, indicate the importance

[27]Davis v. Oregon State Univ., 591 F. 2d 493 (9th Cir. 1978).
[28]Haimowitz v. University of Nevada, 579 F. 2d 526 (9th Cir. 1978).
[29]Evitt v. Monroe, 590 F. Supp. 902 (W.D. Texas 1984).
[30]Jacobs v. College of William and Mary, 495 F. Supp. 183 (E.D. Va. 1980).
[31]Nzomo v, Vermont State Colleges, 385 A. 2d 1099 (Vt. 1978).

of adhering to procedural safeguards whether developed by the institution, required by negotiated agreement or extrapolated from state or federal law.

Notice requirements governing employment may extend beyond provision for notice of adequate cause. For example, while an institution can enforce rules governing outside employment of faculty,[32] the failure to enforce rules governing employment may limit the institution's authority to invoke the rule without notice to faculty. In one instance, the terms of a collective agreement clearly established the institution's authority to prohibit concurrent full-time employment, but the rule was never enforced from its inception in 1969 through 1980. The institution enforced the rule without notice of its intention to do so and acted to dismiss thirty members of the faculty. In upholding a challenge that enforcement of a rule so long dormant was arbitrary and capricious, a federal court insisted that the institution should have notified faculty of intent to implement enforcement in order that faculty could take steps to comply.[33]

However, notice need not strictly conform to institutional regulations where it is reasonable to conclude the employee was adequately informed of charges. A nontenured employee who was given oral notice of termination, contended that the college handbook was incorporated by reference in the annual contract of employment and the handbook compelled written notice of grounds for termination. Although the faculty member had been advised of four specific grounds for termination in a meeting with the college president, and had received a hearing by a special review committee, she insisted that strict adherence to the notice provisions of the handbook was required. The Supreme Court of North Dakota ruled otherwise, finding that the faculty member received adequate notice of the reasons for termination and summarily dismissing her claim that she was denied due process.[34]

The procedural right to a hearing at which the tenured employee may respond to charges prior to dismissal is a guarantee under the due process clause of the Fourteenth Amendment. This hearing cannot be limited by a public institution's procedural standards, although all that is required is a pretermination opportunity to respond to charges, coupled with sufficient posttermination administrative procedures to meet the public institution's guidelines for due process.[35] In general, courts require public institutions to provide some form of

---

[32]See Cook County College Teachers Union v. Board of Trustees, 481 N.E. 2d 40 (Ill. App. 1985).
[33]Kaufman v. Board of Trustees, 552 F. Supp. 1143 (N.D. Ill. 1982).
[34]Stensrud v. Mayville State College, 368 N.W. 2d 519 (N.D. North Dakota 1985).
[35]See Cleveland Bd. of Educ. v. Loudermill, 105 S.Ct. 1487 (1985).

pretermination hearing before a decision dismissing the employee or denying other significant employment benefits can be implemented.[36]

Minimal due process standards include the right to a hearing before an unbiased tribunal at which the employee can refute the allegations related to cause for dismissal and challenge or present evidence and testimony.[37] While the employee cannot compel a rigid checklist of due process protection at the hearing, hearing procedures must be calculated to achieve a fair result, balancing the employee's interest against that of the government so as to avoid any erroneous deprivation of rights.[38] As a consequence, procedural protections at the hearing need not be elaborate or rigidly followed, but they must be responsive to judicial concerns for fairness and impartiality.

Denial of Free Speech, Association or Academic Freedom

While it is undeniable that institutions of higher education have a legitimate interest in discharging unfit employees and in insuring the efficiency of the institution's operations, the right of employees to speak out on matters of public concern or of faculty to exercise authority over matters within the realm of an academic freedom privilege has served as a constraint on these institutional prerogatives. Courts give special scrutiny to dismissal decisions involving the exercise of employee speech, and are particularly sensitive to evidence of pretextual dismissals taken by public institutions in retaliation for an employee's exercise of free speech.

Professional organizations demonstrate a similar sensitivity to free speech issues as related to the concept of academic freedom. The AAUP's "1976 Recommended Institutional Regulations on Academic Freedom and Tenure" states that "adequate cause for a dismissal will be related directly and substantially, to the fitness of the faculty member in his professional capacity as a teacher or researcher. Dismissal will not be used to restrain faculty members in their exercise of academic freedom or other rights of American citizens."[39]

The protection of a public employee's right to speak out on a matter of public concern is a subject of special judicial concern in federal courts. Academic freedom for faculty of public institutions has been characterized by the United States Supreme Court as "a special concern of the First Amendment."[40] However, while these protections are often tied to notions of "academic freedom" it is probably more ac-

---

[36]Skehan v. Board of Trustees of Bloomsburg State College, 501 *F.* 2d 31 (3rd Cir. 1974).
[37]*See* Bowling v. Scott, 587 *F.* 2d 229 (5th Cir. 1979); McLendon v. Morton, 249 *S.E.* 2d 919 (W. Va. 1978); and Poterma v. Ping, 462 *F. Supp.* 388 (E.D. Ohio 1978).
[38]*See* Frumkin v. Board of Trustees of Kent State Univ., 626 *F.* 2d 19 (6th Cir. 1980).
[39]AAUP Policy Documents and Reports, Washington, D.C.: AAUP (1977) at 19.
[40]Keyishian v. Board of Regents, 385 *U.S.* 589, 603 (1967).

curate to characterize these rights as First Amendment constitutional protections, largely because United States courts have been reluctant to recognize an entitlement which would go beyond the grant of free speech and association available to every citizen.

To protect the right of the employee to constitutionally guaranteed First Amendment freedoms, courts have elaborated a series of tests which balance the rights of the individual against the public institution's interest as employer. Typically, an employee would be required to establish that his or her conduct was constitutionally protected, and that it was the exercise of this constitutionally protected right that was the primary or motivating factor in the public institution's decision to deny some employment benefit. Even when an employee could have been discharged for no reason whatever, with no constitutional right to a hearing on the administrative decision, he or she may establish a claim for damages and reinstatement, if the adverse employment decision was made on the basis of the employee's exercise of First Amendment freedoms.

The application of free speech constitutional protections is illustrated in a case involving a non-tenured teacher whose contract was not renewed following her sixth year of teaching in a junior college. The official reason for nonrenewal, "declining enrollment and poor evaluation of work," was appropriate enough, but the faculty member introduced evidence that the real reason for nonrenewal was administrative retaliation for her vigorous support for her husband's candidacy for the college board of regents and her efforts to promote a faculty association. The reviewing federal court noted that the department chairperson and other administrators admitted advising the teacher to have her husband withdraw from the election, voiced objection to her activity on behalf of the teacher's association, and recommended non-renewal to discipline the teacher for trying to create ill will or lack of cooperation with the administration.[41] This evidence supported a jury verdict awarding damages after a finding that the teacher had not been rehired because of her constitutionally protected political and professional activities.[42]

In similar cases involving allegations that an employee was discharged for a constitutionally impermissible reason, courts have relied upon an analytical framework established in a series of United States Supreme Court decisions. This framework requires that courts follow a sequence of four steps in analyzing an employee's free speech claim:

> *First*, did the employee's speech relate to a subject of legitimate public concern, entitling the employee to constitutional protection?

[41]Goss v. San Jacinto Junior College, 588 *F.* 2d 96 (5th Cir. 1979).
[42]*Id.*

42

Second, if protected, was the action taken by the institution in response to the constitutionally protected free speech justified in consideration of the institution's interest in promoting efficiency of operations?

Third, was the employee's protected speech a substantial or motivating factor in the dismissal decision?

Fourth, could the employee be dismissed for adequate cause notwithstanding his exercise of free speech?

In *Connick* v. *Myers,*[43] a governmental employee was terminated after circulating a questionnaire among other employees concerning office policies and morale. The distribution of the questionnaire arose in the context of a dispute between the employee and her supervisor over a transfer and reassignment. The United States Supreme Court reviewed the content of the questionnaire and found it related primarily to matters of personal concern, considering the context of the employee's personal dispute over her reassignment. Since the employee's speech did not relate to a matter of political, social, or other concern to the community, no First Amendment free speech issue was involved and no challenge to the dismissal predicated on a denial of free speech could be sustained by the courts.

In deciding whether a faculty or staff member's free speech rights have been violated, the employee must first carry the burden to establish that the "speech" related to matters of public concern. This initial level of analysis requires the reviewing court to consider the content of the speech and the context in which the speech arose in order to weight the degree of public interest in the employee's speech against the need for effective harmony and discipline required by the public college or university. Under this analysis, an employee's speech or expression could be the basis for an adverse employment decision as long as that speech relates substantially to the employee's personal interests rather than to matters of concern relevant to a political, social, or public policy issue.

The *Connick* analysis was used to justify an adverse employment decision affecting a faculty member who criticized departmental reorganization and allocation of his salary and benefits at a public institution. The critical comments, made to colleagues and students, were held to be matters of individual, not public, concern.[44] The court's opinion included the following pronouncement:

> [A]n individual cannot bootstrap his individual grievance into a matter of public concern by bruiting his complaint to the world or by invoking a supposed popular interest in all aspects of the way public institutions are run.[45]

---

[43]103 *S.Ct.* 1684 (1983).
[44]Mahaffey v. Kansas Bd. of Regents, 562 *F. Supp.* 887 (Kan. 1983).
[45]*Id.* at 890.

Post-*Connick* cases in the public education area assist in understanding the case-by-case analysis involved. In *McGee* v. *South Pemiscott School Dist. R-V*,[46] the court found that a coach's letter to a newspaper concerning the discontinuance of a track program addressed an issue of public concern. Notably, this program discontinuance had been the subject of extensive public controversy and had become an important issue in a pending board election. The context elevated what might under different circumstances have been insignificant content to a public issue.

Presumption of a public controversy also affected a federal court's decision in *Bowman* v. *Pulaski County Spec. School Dist.*,[47] that public statements by assistant coaches concerning their head coach's use of corporal punishment were of public concern. The court took the position that alleged physical mistreatment of students was itself a matter of significant public interest.[48]

Under the *Connick* test, an Ohio counselor's speech was characterized as relating only to her personal interest. Admissions that she was bisexual and had a female lover were made to teaching colleagues on a "confidential" basis, which indicated that she did not consider her comments to be on matters of public concern. Only when she was asked to resign did she talk with other teachers about her sexual preference in an effort to enlist support. These latter statements are particularly like those that went unprotected in *Connick*, because the statements were made in an effort to avoid nonrenewal.[49]

It should not be concluded, however, that merely because a statement is made in private to a fellow employee or superior that that is conclusive on the public concern question. Private statements are accorded First Amendment protection as well.[50]The content of the private speech, such as racial discrimination in the school, can raise an issue of public concern.

In another case relying on the rationale in *Connick*, an Illinois teacher, who was penalized for expressing concern at a board meeting over the operation of a negotiated grievance procedure, prevailed. Other teachers in the school district had expressed concern about the grievance procedure and the board had encouraged teachers to make known any relevant facts about the process. The superintendent could not effectively contend that the teacher was violating a board regulation requiring that any communication from a teacher to a board member must be made through the superintendent, as such a policy

---

[46]712 *F.* 2d 332 (8th Cir. 1983).

[47]723 *F.* 2d 640 (8th Cir. 1983).

[48] *Id.* at 644.

[49]Rowland v. Mad River Dist., 730 *F.* 2d 444 (6th Cir. 1984).

[50]*See Givhan v. Western Line Consol. School Dist.*, 439 *U.S.* 410 (1979).

44

was unconstitutional on its face and in its application to the teacher involved.[51]

Faculty speech on matters of public concern in a public forum has consistently been protected under First Amendment standards unless it could be established that the institution's interest in the efficiency of its operations outweighed the employee's constitutional rights. Faculty legislative lobbying efforts on behalf of higher salaries would appear to be protected speech,[52] as would the expression of unpopular political views[53] and communications disclosing institutional violations of state laws or regulations to proper state authorities.[54] In these and other instances, however, the burden of proof is with the faculty or staff member to establish that the conduct was protected and that the adverse employment decision was primarily or substantially motivated by a desire to punish for that protected conduct.

An avowed Marxist, openly critical of textbooks and politically active on behalf of the Progressive Labor Party, was reinstated by a federal court when it was determined that the administration's ostensible reason for nonrenewal, alleged student complaints, had never been discussed with the professor nor verified by the department chair.[55] After finding that the teacher had never used his classroom to proselytize nor deviated from required curriculum, the court concluded that the teacher's nonrenewal was attributable to his exercise of free speech and held the administration had acted in a constitutionally impermissible fashion.

A professor was denied tenure and discharged after she wrote an editorial for the college paper accusing the chairman of the board of trustees of a conflict of interest in the awarding of a college contract to his nephew. The college president mailed her new contract and congratulated her on receiving tenure. Two months later her new contract was rescinded by the board of trustees because of the alleged impropriety of the editorial. The court held that her discharge was in retaliation for her exercise of protected speech and ordered reinstatement.[56]

In *Pickering* v. *Board of Education*,[57] the Supreme Court found that a teacher's statements, incorporated in a published "letter to the editor" in a local paper, involved a matter of public concern. It pro-

[51]Knapp v. Whitaker, 577 F. Supp. 1265 (C.D. Ill. 1984).
[52]Allaire v. Rogers, 658 F. 2d 1055 (5th Cir. 1981) (faculty lobby for increased salary appropriations before legislature).
[53]Ollman v. Toll, 518 F. Supp. 1196 (D. Md. 1981) aff'med, 704 F. 2d 139 (4th Cir. 1983) (Marxist political views).
[54]Hickingbottom v. Easley, 494 F. Supp. 980 (E.D. Ark. 1980) (letter disclosing improper licensing of university president's automobile).
[55]Cooper v. Ross, 472 F. Supp. 802 (E.D. Pa. 1979).
[56]Endress v. Brookdale Community College, 364 A. 2d 1080 (N.J. Sup. 1976).
[57]391 U.S. 563 (1968).

ceeded to set out the method by which a court is to determine if a public employee's free speech right has been violated by the response of his employer.

The court recognized that a governmental body acting as an employer has a greater interest in regulating the acts of its employees than it does with respect to the public at large.[58] This interest derives from the need to promote efficiency and integrity in operations and to maintain appropriate discipline. As a result, a decision rests on weighing the relative interests of the teacher and the school district. This test requires a court to find:

> [A] balance between the interests of the [employee], as a citizen, in commenting upon matters of public concern and the interest of the state, as an employer, in promoting the efficiency of the public services it performs through its employees.[59]

Once the employee establishes that his or her speech was protected, the college or university must establish that its action was justified in the interest of effective and efficient performance of its responsibilities. The focus is on the effect of the employee's conduct within the working environment. Particularly relevant are the effect of the protected conduct on a faculty member's ability to perform, relationships with other employees and resulting disruption of institutional operation.

Once the employee has established that he engaged in conduct protected under the First Amendment, he must prove that this conduct was a substantial or motivating factor in the adverse employment action taken by the school district.[60] If this burden is carried, the district may prove, by a preponderance of the evidence, that it would have reached the same decision even in the absence of the protected conduct.[61] The sum of these shifting burdens of proof is that the evidence must show that *but for* the protected conduct the teacher would not have been subject to the adverse employment action.[62]

The rationale behind the *but for* standard is that the constitutional principle requires no more than that the employee be placed in no worse position than if he had not engaged in the protected conduct. This reduces the possibility that an employee could, by engaging in offensive but protected conduct, preclude his employer from terminating or disciplining him for other, possibly preexisting, reasons unrelated to the exercise of the free speech right.

Institutions of higher education can withstand a charge of denying free speech and association if it can be shown that the faculty or

---

[58]*Id.* at 568.
[59]*Id.*
[60]Mt Healthy Bd. of Educ. v. Doyle, 429 *U.S.* 278, 287 (1979).
[61]*Id.*
[62]Givhan, 439 *U.S.* at 417.

staff member could have been disciplined notwithstanding the exercise of constitutionally protected rights. A jury verdict for an institution was affirmed on appeal when the court held that the teacher was denied salary increases due to unsatisfactory scholarship rather than public criticism of university projects.[63] In a similar case, a university dean's affidavit established that a professor was denied summer teaching and given a relatively small salary increase in order that the lowest paid faculty members might be provided additional compensation as an inducement to keep highly competent but underpaid young faculty.[64] The affidavit overcame the senior faculty member's allegations that the denial of salary increases and summer teaching was in retaliation for the professor's opposition to the dean's selection during search committee deliberations.

When a faculty member was not renewed after protesting reassignment from a graduate to a freshman course, he challenged the department chairman's recommendation not to renew on the basis that his criticism of the chairman's directive on reassignment was protected by free speech. However, the record supported the testimony of the department head that the decision not to renew had been reached some months prior to the teacher's protests and criticisms of the department chairman and the court concluded that the decision not to renew was not predicated on the faculty member's exercise of free speech.[65]

A tenured assistant professor, dismissed for playing a prominent role in unauthorized protest activities which took place during school hours on school property, contended that his dismissal was in retaliation for his exercise of free speech and assembly rights granted by the constitution. The facts were that the professor tried to stop a motorcade bringing officials to a campus ceremony, led student demonstrators in raucous catcalls to disrupt the ceremonies, and encouraged demonstrators out of their seats and onto the stadium field, thus creating a danger of violent confrontation. The court upheld a finding that the professor's actions went beyond advocacy of ideas, counseling and engaging in a course of conduct which interfered and disrupted the regular operation of the school in a manner which left him outside the protection of the First Amendment.[66]

Where protected speech or academic freedom issues relate to conduct in the classroom, courts have demonstrated considerable reluctance to intervene in adverse employment decisions. A nontenured faculty member who was not reviewed because her teaching philosophy conflicted with the pedagogical approach favored by the institution failed to establish a violation of free speech or academic freedom related

[63]Berry v. Battey, 666 F. 2d 1183 (8th Cir. 1981).
[64]Stone v. Regents, 620 F. 2d 526 (5th Cir. 1980).
[65]Hillis v. Stephen F. Austin State Univ., 665 F. 2d 547 (5th Cir. 1982).
[66]Adamian v. Lombardi, 608 F. 2d 1224 (9th Cir. 1979).

to her choice of teaching methods.[67] Similarly, a substitute teacher who was not continued because his methods of teaching and counseling were at variance with the curriculum and procedures at the state university did not establish that his activities were matters of public concern justifying constitutional protection.[68]

However, a public college or university must be cautious in undertaking employment actions which would restrict a faculty member's free speech or academic freedom rights related to classroom speech on controversial yet curriculum-related issues. An administrative reprimand for speaking out on a college collective bargaining controversy in a political science class could be considered a violation of free speech and academic freedom if it were established that the topic was a matter of public concern relevant to the curriculum and the reprimand had a "chilling effect" on free speech by creating an atmosphere in which the action was viewed as a sanction for faculty speech on controversial yet germane topics.[69]

Courts have acknowledged that a public college or university employee will not be immunized against an adverse employment decision involving noncooperative, unprofessional or insubordinate conduct simply by invoking the protections of the First Amendment.[70] An assistant professor who was denied tenure contended that the department chairman's unfavorable recommendation on tenure was an attempt to punish for the professor's criticism of the chair. Even assuming that this activity might be constitutionally protected, the reviewing federal appeals court found considerable evidence to justify denial of tenure based upon unfavorable annual evaluations, complaints relating to the assistant professor's refusal to teach courses in a manner consistent with the adopted curriculum and reports of contentious behavior with colleagues.[71]

The dean of instruction at a community college was not protected by a free speech right in his public criticism of the college president. The president acted to dismiss the dean for insubordination and unprofessional conduct, and the college board moved to dismiss following a notice of charges and a hearing. On judicial review, the federal district court found the statements not constitutionally protected. Concluding that the statements carried threats of hostility and physical violence, the court affirmed dismissal on the basis that the comments were unprofessional and interfered with harmonious relations necessary for institutional operation.[72]

---

[67]Hetrick v. Martin, 480 F. 2d 705 (6th Cir. 1973).

[68]Clark v. Holmes, 474 F. 2d 928 (7th Cir. 1972).

[69]Mahoney v. Hankin, 593 F. Supp. 1171 (E.D. 1984).

[70]See Kelly v. Kansas Community College, 648 P. 2d 225 (Kansas 1982); Stastny v. Board of Trustees, 647 P. 2d 496 (Wash App. 1982); and Jawa v. Fayetteville State Univ., 426 F. Supp. 218 (E.D. N.C. 1976).

[71]Mayberry v. Dees, 663 F. 2d 502 (4th Cir. 1981).

[72]Russ v. White, 541 F. Supp. 888 (W.D.Ark.1981). See McCain v.Commw. Dept.of Educ., 454 A. 2d 667 (Pa. Commw. 1983) (suspension for alleging superior was incompetent).

Discrimination

Discrimination on the basis of race, religion, national origin, sex, age or handicap is prohibited under federal law and the provisions of many state laws, most of which are applicable to both public and private institutions of higher education.[73] Since the litigation of employment discrimination claims is highly fact intensive, documentation of employee dismissal should be designed to provide a strong evidentiary basis for rebutting a claim of discrimination. Nothing can prevent charges of discrimination from arising, but summary disposition of the charges will be more likely where employment practices include documentary records which support a strong anti-discrimination posture.[74]

The primary constitutional and statutory provisions governing issues of employment discrimination in dismissal cases focus on the equal protection clause of the Fourteenth Amendment, Title VII of the Civil Rights Act of 1964, and Title IX of the Education Amendments of 1972. In recent years, faculty and staff alleging a discriminatory intent on the part of colleges and universities have relied on the provisions of Title VII rather than on the rigorous proof of *dejure* intent to discriminate required under the Fourteenth Amendment or on the as yet unresolved standards to be used in Title IX proceedings.

Title VII of the Civil Rights Act of 1964 prohibits employment discrimination against individuals on the basis of race, color, religion, sex, or national origin.[75] Employment practices which result in disparate treatment of a person or class protected by the act constitute one form of discrimination; however, the employer can justify disparate treatment by articulating a legitimate, non-discriminatory reason for the employment decision, such as an occupational qualification which bears a reasonable relationship to the job in question.[76]

Overt discrimination in employment decision-making is one of the most obvious forms of discrimination prohibited by Title VII. Legal controversy in most of these cases has alternated between the employee's burden to establish a prima facie case and the defendant employer's burden to articulate some legitimate nondiscriminatory reason for the allegedly discriminatory practice. In instances in which "disparate treatment" is alleged, the ultimate factual inquiry is whether the employer or its agents intentionally discriminated against the

---

[73]*See, for example,* 42 U.S.C. §2000(e) (1976) (Title VII of the 1964 Civil Rights Act); 20 U.S.C. §1681 (1976) (Title IX of the Education Amendments of 1972); and 29 U.S.C. §794 (1976) (Section 504 of the Rehabilitation Act of 1973).

[74]Evidence an institution has developed and is implementing an affirmative action plan is relevant to questions of discriminatory intent. *See* Craik v. University of Minnesota, 731 F. 2d 465 (8th Cir. 1984).

[75]42 U.S.C. §2000(e).

[76]Texas Dept. of Community Affairs v. Burdine, 450 *U.S.* 248 (1981).

individual.[77] While such a proof rests with the person bringing the claim, a claimant must meet a limited initial burden of proof. After this initial showing, the court will require the employer to articulate a legitimate nondiscriminatory reason for the hiring practice. If the employer meets this burden of proof, the claimant must go forward with a showing that the articulated reason is a pretext masking the employer's actual discriminatory intent.

This shifting burden of proof involves a three-step process. *First*, the plaintiff has the burden of proving, by a preponderance of the evidence, a prima facie case of discrimination. This may be accomplished by evidence that the plaintiff was a member of the protected group, and was dismissed under circumstances permitting an inference of discrimination. *Second*, if the plaintiff has established a prima facie case, the burden of producing evidence shifts to the defendant "to articulate some legitimate, nondiscriminatory reason for the employee's rejection."[78] *Third*, should the defendant carry this burden, the plaintiff may offer evidence that the defendant's ostensibly legitimate reasons were not genuinely held but were merely a pretext for discrimination. While the test does shift the burden of production once a plaintiff has offered a prima facie case, the burden of persuasion remains upon the plaintiff at all times.[79]

As previously noted, employment practices based upon subjective criteria are often closely scrutinized by courts because of the potential for masking unlawful discrimination. While the use of subjective criteria may not necessarily give rise to a *per se* finding of discriminatory intent,[80] it is highly probable that the college or university will be compelled to detail its documentation system and establish that criteria were job-related and employment practices were uniformly applied. Further, the institution must articulate the rationale for dismissal decisions in a manner which will lend credence to the view that no discriminatory animus influenced the process.[81] An institution's failure to apply uniform employment procedures and submit evidence of reasonable comparisons between employees may implicate a disparate treatment claim. In one instance, evidence of an abrupt change in teacher evaluation ratings coupled with statistical evidence of a disparity in the number of black employees in a school district was held sufficient to justify a determination that the district discriminated against a black physical education teacher. Most comments evaluating the teacher were favorable until just before the determination on tenure, and there were only two black teachers out of 281 employed in the

---

[77]McDonnell Douglas Corp. v. Green, 411 *U.S.* 792 (1973).

[78]*Id.* 802.

[79]Burdine, 450 *U.S.* 248.

[80]*See* Love v. Alamance County Bd. of Educ., 581 *F. Supp.* 1079 (M.D. N.C. 1984).

[81]*See* Parker v. Board of School Comm'rs of Indianapolis, 729 *F.* 2d 524 (7th Cir. 1984).

district. The New York appeal's court enjoined further discriminatory practice in the district, reinstated the teacher to a probationary position, and required the district to afford the employee a fair and non-discriminatory tenure evaluation.[82]

In another case which involved the lack of uniform evaluation processes, a teacher established that she was a victim of sex discrimination when she was denied a position as an administrator. In selecting a male candidate for the position, the board emphasized attributes such as "tact," "ability to deal with others," and "character" as factors weighed in favor of the male, but failed to demonstrate that they had asked whether the female applicant had comparable qualities. This failure to compare the qualities of the applicants, coupled with a history of selecting male applicants for administrative positions over a twenty-five year period, was sufficient to establish that there was substantial evidence of sex discrimination.[83]

Black teachers successfully contested non-reappointment decisions by demonstrating that the evaluation process on which nonrenewals were based was not uniformly applied to all teaching personnel. In the year prior to voluntary desegregation of the district, black teachers were twice singled out for evaluation and eight of the total number of twenty-three black teachers were numerically ranked. When the plan for desegregation was implemented, seventeen black teachers were not renewed, although all white teachers in the district were offered new contracts. When seventeen new teachers were hired, all seventeen were white. The Fifth Circuit Court of Appeals concluded the nonrenewals were intentional acts of racial discrimination and noted that the separate evaluation and ranking of black teachers was highly probative although circumstantial evidence of unconstitutional discrimination.[84]

Evaluations which reflect an emphasis on sexual or racial sterotyping also implicate disparate treatment claims. An evaluation process which expressly presumes that males are better suited to administrative or managerial roles would constitute sex discrimination under Title VII.[85] Evidence of an administrator's attitudinal disposition prejudicial to a protected class of individuals would most certainly call into question an adverse employment decision.[86] Testimony indicating a preference for white applicants for a position as a staff member would suggest discriminatory animus in the assessment and selection process.[87]

---

[82]Guilderland Central School Dist. v. New York State Human Rights Appeal Bd., 461 N.Y.S. 2d 599 (App. Div. 1983).

[83]Strand v. Petersburg Public Schools, 659 P. 2d 1218 (Alaska, 1983).

[84]Harkless v. Sweeney Independent School Dist., 554 F. 2d 1353 (5th Cir. 1977).

[85]See Coble v. Hot Springs School Dist., 682 F. 2d 721 (8th Cir. 1982).

[86]See Padway v. Palches, 665 F. 2d 965 (9th Cir. 1982).

[87]Stafford v. Muscogee County Bd. of Educ., 688 F. 2d 1838 (11th Cir. 1982).

The principal case involving disparate treatment in higher education is *Board of Trustees of Keene State College* v. *Sweeney*,[88] a case which involved allegations of sex discrimination in the denial of promotion to a female associate professor. Dr. Sweeney was successful in establishing a prima facie case of sex discrimination by a statistical showing that the promotion of women at Keene was substantially confined to the lower ranks. The college sought to demonstrate that its decision not to promote Sweeney to full professor was based upon legitimate factors, citing insufficient service to the college, primarily in committee work, and personality considerations which allegedly interfered with her teaching and relationships with colleagues. The United States Supreme Court ruled that once the college articulated a legitimate non-discriminatory basis for its adverse employment decision, the burden of proof shifted once again to Dr. Sweeney, who must establish that the articulated reason offered by the college was a subterfuge or pretext for a discriminatory practice.[89] Sweeney carried this burden. She demonstrated that her complaints concerning discrimination had largely been ignored by the administration and that the "personality variables" which were a basis for denial of promotion had not been introduced when she was granted tenure at the college two years previous to the initial denial of promotion. Sweeney had been promoted to full professor two years after the initial denial of promotion. The reasons cited for promotion emphasized her committee service, excellence in teaching and community service, factors which had been cited as negative performance indicators during the initial promotion decision, yet Dr. Sweeney's qualifications had not changed in any significant way in the interim between promotion decisions.

Disparate treatment in the *Sweeney* case was manifest in administrative indifference to the concerns of women faculty, statistically significant differences in hiring and promotion practices, inconsistent application of promotion and tenure criteria and a preoccupation with trivial criticisms as a justification for employment decisions.

In another case, disparate treatment was established by a showing that a female faculty member was evaluated for tenure using criteria different from those applied to similarly situated male candidates and that personnel advisement practices discriminated on the basis of sex within the department.[90] Similarly, a department chairman's imposition of degree requirements not initially required nor reasonably related to a position as athletic administrator and coach were held to be evidence of a discriminatory animus.[91]

---

[88]604 *F.* 2d 106 (1st Cir. 1979), *cert denied,* 444 *U.S.* 1045 (1980).
[89]Board of Trustees of Keene State College v. Sweeney, 439 *U.S.* 24 (1978).
[90]Kunda v. Muhlenberg College, 621 *F.* 532 (3rd Cir. 1980).
[91]Hill v. Nettleton, 455 *F. Supp.* 514 (D. Colo. 1978).

Once an employee establishes a prima facie case of discrimination, the college or university must demonstrate that its employment decision (whether related to hiring, promotion, award of tenure or benefits, demotion or termination) is based upon legitimate factors and not on explicit or implicit considerations prohibited by Title VII. Such a proposition does not rule out peer review, nor does it hold that considerations of teaching, research and service (utilizing essentially subjective criteria) are inappropriate to the employment decision. What is important is that there be no differential treatment in the employment decision making process. Uniformity in the application of procedures and standards for evaluation are essential. The articulation of a rationale for employment decisions that bears a reasonable relationship to departmental, college and institutional objectives is extremely important. The articulated basis for adverse employment decisions should relate to legitimate, performance-related reasons, which might include negative student evaluations, unwillingness to assume responsibility for teaching or service assignments, refusal to accept student advisers, and the like.

Uniform and non-discriminatory evaluation processes may often be relied upon to rebut a claim of employment discrimination. In one case, use of a four-step evaluation procedure incorporating self-evaluation, observations and evaluation by colleagues followed by a conference emphasizing methods to improve performance and a second evaluation by faculty colleagues when low ratings had been received was challenged by a nonrenewed black teacher. The appellate court affirmed the trial court's view that the evaluation process was neither facially discriminatory nor unreasonably burdensome to the black teacher and was an appropriate basis on which to predicate the adverse employment decision.[92]

Although initially successful in establishing a prima facie claim of sex discrimination, a part-time teacher lost her *pro se* appeal from a decision dismissing her claim with prejudice. In response to plaintiff's initial proof of discrimination, defendants presented what the trial court described as "over whelming" evidence that the denial of a position to the teacher was free of unlawful discrimination. The evaluative record established that the teacher had been a disruptive rather than contributive factor in the system, and the trial court found that the teacher was denied renewal because of her unwillingness to observe rules and regulations, failure to work harmoniously with other staff and refusal to submit documentation essential to her employment. Finding no error, the Eighth Circuit Court of Appeals affirmed.[93]

In two cases involving dismissal for insubordination, school employees were unsuccessful in establishing claims of sex discrimina-

[92]Pickens v. Okolona Municipal Separate School dist., 527 F. 2d 358 (5th Cir. 1976).
[93]Scharnhorst v. Independent School Dist. No. 710, 686 F. 2d 637 (8th Cir. 1982).

tion under Title VII. A female coach in Illinois refused to comply with her superior's request to have some students temporarily vacate lockers in the girls' locker room. The teacher sought to establish a prima facie case of sex discrimination by alleging that she was dismissed for insubordination while her male superior was not disciplined, that no investigation of her grievance over the incident had been undertaken by school authorities, and that the school district employed more male than female coaches. These allegations were not considered sufficient to raise an inference of discrimination in her dismissal.[94] Similarly, a black female counselor in South Carolina who interfered with a reading test administration on the basis that no notice had been given to her students, failed to establish a prima facie case of sex discrimination particularly when the record established that the counselor had repeatedly refused to explain her actions to superiors.[95]

An institution of higher education has overcome a prima facie case of discriminatory discharge under Title VII through documentation of an employee's poor work habits, discord with superiors, and inadequate productivity.[96] In another case, the institution met its burden to overcome a claim of discrimination in staff promotion practices by setting forth objective criteria related to advanced degree requirements that were shown to be reasonably related to the requirements for the position.[97] In a third instance, a community college's composite evaluation system for award of promotion and sabbatical leave, though scored subjectively by faculty peers, was enough to overcome an inference of discrimination advanced by a female black faculty member.[98]

Breach of Contract

Courts require both public and private institutions to comply with institutional procedures which are part of the employment contract or incorporated as part of the terms of employment. If a college policy statement providing a right to notice and hearing is recognized as an employee's contractual right, then the institution can be held accountable for breach of that agreement if it fails to meet the obligation.[99] Since private colleges are not subject to the constitutional constraints applicable to public institutions, common law contract, or tort precepts[100] may be the principal basis for establishing an employee's legal claim.[101]

---

[94]Kneeland v. Bloom Twp. High School Dist., 518 *F. Supp.* 890 (N.D. Ill. 1981).

[95]Moore v. Bonner, 526 *F. Supp.* 143 (D.S.C. 1981).

[96]Lewis v. University of Pittsburg, 725 *F.* 2d 910 (3rd Cir. 1984). *See also* Balicao v. University of Minnesota, 737 *F.* 2d 747 (8th Cir. 1984).

[97]Sweeney v. Research Foundation of State Univ., 711 *F.* 2d 1179 (2nd Cir. 1983).

[98]Walton v. St. Louis Community College, 587 *F. Supp.* 458 (E.D. Mo. 1984).

[99]Skehan v. Board of Trustees of Bloomsburg State College, 501 *F.* 2d 31 (3rd Cir. 1976).

[100]For a discussion of emerging tort law theories which appear to be gaining credence in the dissmisal of at-will employees, See Hustoles, "Faculty and Staff Dismissals: Developing Contract and Tort Theories," 10 *J. C. and Univ. L.* 479-494 (1983).

[101]*See* Johnson v. Christain Brothers College, 565 *S.W.* 2d 872 (Tenn. 1978).

In defining the employee's contractual rights, courts can look to verbal promises or assurances by institutional agents, institutional policy statements governing employment, and traditional custom or practice. The decision to go beyond the contract as written is often predicated on a judge's attempt to resolve material ambiguities in the employment agreement or to determine what portions of an agreement are enforceable. A California appeals court went beyond the contract of employment and the regulatory policies of the regents in considering custom and conditions unique to a faculty member funded through a research grant.[102] Finding that the employee had been unfairly treated in the decision to terminate, the court ordered the university to reconsider its adverse employment decision in recognition of a faculty committee's finding that the professor was entitled to continuity of employment so long as the grant funds were available.[103]

While courts generally adhere to the express terms of a written agreement, contracts of employment in colleges or universities have consistently been interpreted to "comprehend as essential parts of themselves the hiring policies and practices of the university as embodied in its employment regulations and customs."[104] Thus, the usual practices of the institution surrounding the contractual relationship can become the contractual obligation of the institution.[105]

Typically, courts construing external documents, custom and usage in higher education contracts of employment are involved in determinations of whether the employee can rely on automatic renewal of contract or award of tenure. A judicially affirmed expectation of continued employment has been predicated on a failure to give reasonable notice of non-renewal where institutional regulations or state statutes provided for automatic renewal of a teacher's contract in the absence of timely notice.[106] A handbook provision providing three years probation after which a teacher would be employed on continuing contract with dismissal only for incompetence or disruptive conduct created a legitimate contractual expectation of tenure after the faculty member had been employed five years.[107]

In cases involving wrongful discharge, private and public institutions are presented with the prospect that the employee will argue contract modifications based upon institutional policies, oral assurances, and/or custom and practice. Since these contentions involve findings

---

[102]Adelson v. Regents of the University of California, 180 *Cal. Rptr.* 676 (Cal. App. 1982).
[103]*Id.* at 679.
[104]Greene v. Howard Univ., 412 *F.* 2d 1128, 1135 (D.C. App. 1969).
[105]*See* Bason v. American Univ., 414 *A.* 2d 522 (D.C. 1980); Pride v. Howard Univ., 484 *A.* 2d 31 (D.C. 1978); and Perry v. Sindermann, 408 *U.S.* 593 (1971).
[106]*See* Pima College v. Sinclair, 496 *P.* 2d 639 (Ariz. App. 1972); Davis v. Board of Educ. of Harrison, 342 *N.W.* 2d 528 (Mich. App. 1983). *But see* Smith v. Green, 545 *P.* 2d 550 (Wash. 1976).
[107]Thomas v. Ward, 529 *F.* 2d 916 (4th Cir. 1975).

of law and fact, the resolution of ambiguous contract terms can be a significant source of litigation. As virtually every act or omission of the institution can serve as a basis for "custom" or "usage," institutions should make reasonable efforts to specify standards applicable to the faculty or staff member's employment status and periodically notify employees of that status. In particular, non-tenured and at-will employees of the institution should be apprised of their status and reminded of applicable policy and provisions governing that status.

Chapter IV

Conclusions

Despite the high incidence of litigation involving dismissal for cause, courts generally adopt a deferential attitude toward institutional authority to effect adverse employment decisions. Where colleges and universities have published standards that guide employment practices related to dismissal for cause, courts typically grant wide discretion to the institution in determining the meaning and intent of those standards while insisting upon substantial compliance with the procedural requirements for enforcing standards. Courts are clearly guardians of procedure, reluctant to invade the substantive decision making process of academic governance even when sensitive issues of employee dismissal are involved.

Noting that "the competence of teachers and the standards of its measurement are not, without more, matters of constitutional dimensions,"[1] one federal appeals court rejected a faculty member's claims of arbitrary treatment. In related cases involving institutional decisions to refuse tenure or deny contract renewal, judges have emphasized that institutional employment practices are peculiarly the province of institutional decision makers, subject to limited review by courts.

Courts consistently acknowledge that dismissals of tenured postsecondary faculty are within the competence and authority of college and university administrators. The deferential attitude of courts is particularly apparent in a New York judicial opinion:

> The management of the university is primarily the responsibility of those equipped with the special skills and sensitivities necessary for so delicate a task. One of the most sensitive functions of the university administration is the appointment, promotion, and retention of the faculty. It is for this reason that the courts, and admin-

---

[1]Brouillette v. Board of Directors, 519 F. 2d 126, 131 (8th Cir. 1975).

istrative agencies as well, should only rarely assume academic oversight, except with the greatest caution and restraint, in such sensitive areas as faculty appointment, promotion, and tenure, especially in institutions of higher learning.[2]

While the level of judicial scrutiny applicable to a college or university's dismissal of an employee will vary, courts are unlikely to interfere when the adverse employment decision is based upon criteria reasonably related to job requirements and ostensibly free of impermissible discrimination or the denial of a constitutional right to free speech or association. If determinations made by the college or university's academic agencies are reached by proper procedures and supported by substantial evidence, judges are unlikely to interfere. Judicial intervention would necessitate review of a host of factors used by educators to make employment decisions, a role courts have neither the competency nor the resources to undertake.[3]

Nevertheless, if responsible administrators do not have reasoned, ascertainable standards for making adverse employment decisions, or if they fail to apply those standards in a particular employment decision, the consequences may implicate legally protectable rights and result in legal challenge. Judicial review of the employment decision making processes can be anticipated when employment decisions appear arbitrary or capricious, lack supporting evidence, or deny the individual's legally protected rights.

Sound employment practices provide a record of events, incidents, appraisals, discussions, interviews, and admonitions which can be relied upon to support the evidentiary sufficiency and credibility of an employment decision involving professional personnel. When efforts to improve performance have failed and an adverse employment decision is compelled, that decision must be predicated upon standards reasonably related to job requirements and upon careful adherence to the procedural requirements established by law, contract, or institutional policy.

To withstand judicial scrutiny amid the formidable array of legal constraints on the dismissal of professional employees, three steps are in order. *First*, the institution must determine, in advance, the job-related competencies it requires of its professional personnel. *Second*, the system must implement mechanisms for identifying deficiencies related to the competencies it has specified. *Third*, the professional employee must be adequately informed of the competencies he or she must meet and provided with a reasonable opportunity to correct remediable deficiencies once identified.

---

[2]New York Inst. of Technology v. State Division of Human Rights, 386 *N.Y.S.* 2d 685, 688 (N.Y. 1976).
[3]*See* Kramedas v. Board of Educ., 523 *F. Supp.* 1263 (D. Del. 1981).

It is recommended that faculty and professional staff of the institution be included in the process of establishing professional competencies and encouraged to participate in every phase of the employment decision making process. From policy formulation to implementation, employee participation in employment decision making enhances employee relations, provides for more informed decision making and contributes to a perception of fundamental fairness and reasonableness that can deter law suits and reduce judicial intervention.[4]

Once the institution identifies competencies for job performance, it must establish mechanisms which periodically assess employee performance and allow for review and record keeping necessary to the documentation process. Such a documentation process is essential to reliable and valid employment decisions. Furthermore, a documentation system at each stage of the employment decision making process will insure accountability and reduce allegations of arbitrary and capricious action or bad faith in adverse employment decisions.

Procedures for the evaluation of employee performance and review of employment decision making should be clearly articulated and uniformly applied. All employees should be periodically apprised of procedures applicable to personnel administration through annual publication of a handbook and periodic dissemination of special memoranda. Uniform application of the procedures for handling employment decisions is essential to avoid threshold due process challenges to an adverse employment decision.

Development and implementation of legally sound employment practices and procedures will not eliminate legal disputes, but should yield a documentary record which substantiates the fairness and reasonableness of the process, establishes the proper predicate for an adverse employment decision, and elaborates the procedural integrity of the process. Evaluative criteria must be developed which, though often subjective, are sufficiently specific and reasonably job-related to enable the employee to guide his or her conduct and provide a standard by which the employee's conduct can be evaluated.[5] Systematic and uniform application of those criteria must characterize the process that will ultimately be relied upon to support employment decisions. *Finally*, employment practices must be procedurally correct, whether that procedure is express or implicit in the provisions of due process of law.

[4]*See* Hendrickson and Lee, *Academic Employment and Retrenchment: Judicial Review and Administrative Action* (1983).
[5]*See* Lee, "Heightened Performance Standards for Faculty," *West's Education L. Rptr.*

Appendix I

Resources for Legal Information in Secondary and Higher Education

MONOGRAPHS

If you have found the information contained in this monograph to be helpful in your day-to-day operations and as a reference it is quite likely that you may also be interested in other titles included in the *The Higher Education Administration Series* or in our publications that offer quarterly updates on case law related to various fields of education.

Following is a list of titles available from College Administration Publications. Where the titles are not illustrative of the subject covered, a brief description is included. If you wish to order, there is an order blank on the reverse side of this sheet which you may wish to copy rather than tearing out this page.

Other titles in *The Higher Education Administration Series:*

☐ Administering College and University Housing:
A Legal Perspective

☐ The Dismissal of Students with Mental Disorders:
Legal Issues, Policy Considerations
and Alternative Responses

☐ Computers in Education:
Legal Liabilities and Ethical Issues
Concerning Their Use and Misuse

☐ A Practical Guide to Legal Issues Affecting College Teachers

PERIODICALS

The following publications offer the reader a quarterly report on recent precedent setting higher court decisions covering a wide range of subjects in the area encompassed by the self-descriptive title. In addition, through the accumulated back issues, and in the "College" publications, a casebook, each of these publications are also excellent comprehensive references that can be of great help in day-to-day operations and long range planning:

▶ The College Student and the Courts
▶ The College Administrator and the Courts
▶ The Schools and the Courts

While primarily written for practicing administrators, superintendents, school boards, teachers and legal counsel in secondary education, this publication is of great value to related schools of education.

61

Order Blank

Bill to:............................. Ship to:............................

....

....

| Quantity | Item & Price | Total |

MONOGRAPHS

_____ **The Dismissal of Students with Mental Disorders:**
1 to 9 copies @ $9.95; 10 or more copies @ $9.50 _____

_____ **Administering College and University Housing:**
·1 to 9 copies @ $9.95; 10 or more copies @ $9.50 _____

_____ **A Practical Guide to Legal Issues Affecting
College Teachers**
1 to 9 copies @ $4.95; 10 to 24 copies @ $3.95;
25 or more copies @ $3.50 _____

_____ **Computers in Education:
Legal Liabilities and Ethical Issues
Concerning Their Use and Misuse**
1 to 9 copies @ $9.95; 10 or more copies @ $9.50 _____

_____ **Faculty / Staff Nonrenewal and Dismissal for Cause
in Institutions of Higher Education**
1 to 9 copies @ $9.95; 10 or more copies @ $9.50 _____

PERIODICALS

_____ **The College Student and the Courts**
Includes casebook, all back issues and four
quarterly updating supplements.............$98.50 _____

_____ **The College Administrator and the Courts**
Includes casebook, all back issues and four
quarterly updating supplements.............$77.50 _____

_____ **The Schools and the Courts**
Includes over 600 pages of back issues and four
updating reports...........................$67.50 _____

*Postage (if payment accompanies
order we will ship postpaid)* _____

North Carolina residents add appropriate sales tax _____

Total _____

Address Orders to:
College Administration Publications, Inc.
Dept. FD, P.O. Box 8492, Asheville, NC 28814

☐ Pricing of the above publications was correct on the publication
date of this monograph. If you wish to be advised of current prices
of titles you have ordered before shipment, please check.

☐ For further information regarding any of the above titles please
indicate with check here and in the quantity column of each publication and we will forward current brochures and information.

PHOTOCOPY OR DETACH AND MAIL

NOTES

NOTES

NOTES

NOTES

NOTES

NOTES

NOTES

NOTES